## PRAISE FOR *THE HUNGER*

"*The Hunger* is perhaps the most accurate description of the careers of many chefs these days. DeLucie was a journeyman until the gods of fortune smiled upon him with a business partner named Graydon Carter, whose *Vanity Fair* Rolodex ensured a packed and illustrious dining room from Day One at their restaurant, The Waverly Inn."

—*Los Angeles Times*

"This dishy read is an insider's look at what it takes to stay on top of the high-pressure, high-profile culinary world and what really goes on in the kitchen."

—*Bon Appétit*

"It's the rare behind-the-scenes glimpses into the Waverly's clubby quarters that make this book different from other chef memoirs and their typically debauched tales."

—*New York Post*

"When word gets out that chef John DeLucie is doing some of the best tuna tartar in town (all of that creamy avocado and zingy heat!), plus a hefty and juicy pork chop, a classically blissful Dover sole, an addictive clam chowder, a gorgeous fillet of wild salmon (with those adorable little beluga lentils), and such feloniously fatty short ribs, won't there even be more lemmings tumbling down the steps from Bank Street and through the door?"

—Frank Bruni, *New York Times*

"DeLucie provides an excellent balance of personal details and authentic backstage culinary tales. . . . DeLucie's is a satisfying triumph of hard work and stick-to-it-ness."     —*Publishers Weekly*

"His portraits of the unique personalities that inhabit the kitchen are delightful, and his emphasis on the teamwork and leadership required to run a successful restaurant is inspiring. Though there are celebrity-driven anecdotes sprinkled throughout the text, the story never becomes gossipy. . . . A colorful vignette of New York's cutthroat culinary scene by a qualified insider."     —*Kirkus Reviews*

"John DeLucie has given me so much pleasure at The Waverly Inn, and now he has written this delightful book as well! I recommend it to anyone interested in good food—and good stories."     —Salman Rushdie

"Hot grease, sharp knives, infidelity, and white truffles. . . . *The Hunger* has all the right ingredients. John DeLucie has lived the life and now he tells the tale. *The Hunger* is the best memoir by a chef since *Kitchen Confidential*."     —Jay McInerney

"In a bowl, stir gently, one part Hard Work, two cups True Grit, and a dash of Restaurant Glamour, and you get the perfect recipe for chef John DeLucie's everyday life. *The Hunger* is a firsthand account about what it's like to manage kitchen chaos, dining room politics, and, oh yeah . . . a personal life! I couldn't put it down."     —Bobby Flay

"*The Hunger* entertainingly describes one of those wonderfully unlikely bizarro career arcs that can only happen in the restaurant business, a journey peopled with the usual suspects from The Life: crackpots, geniuses, artists, and douche bags, the famous, the fabulous, and the cold-blooded professionals. A terrific first-person tour of the best and worst of the back-of-the-house New York restaurant world with an all-too-rare happy ending." —Anthony Bourdain

"John DeLucie captures all of the tangy Dostoyevskian world of food and restaurants in his magnificent and tasty memoir. *The Hunger* is as funny as Robin Williams, as sharp as a good vinaigrette, and as satisfying as lasagna Bolognese—a must-read for foodies and for fans of the new food culture—and those obsessed with it—as well as the characters who make it." —Mario Batali

ecco

*An Imprint of HarperCollinsPublishers*

# THE HUNGER

## A MEMOIR OF AN
## ACCIDENTAL CHEF

# JOHN DeLUCIE

HarperCollins books may be purchased for educational, business, or sales promotional use. For information, please write: Special Markets Department, HarperCollins Publishers, 10 East 53rd Street, New York, NY 10022.

A hardcover edition of this book was published in 2009 by Ecco, an imprint of HarperCollins Publishers.

FIRST ECCO PAPERBACK EDITION 2010

*Designed by Suet Y. Chong*

Title page photograph by Maren Caruso/Getty Images

Library of Congress Cataloging-in-Publication Data is available upon request.

ISBN: 978-0-06-157929-5

10 11 12 13 14   OV/RRD   10 9 8 7 6 5 4 3 2

*To Mom and Dad*

# Acknowledgments

Many years ago my good friend Ken Carlton and I were wasting away an afternoon in a Greenwich Village café, drinking coffee and reminiscing about old times. We knew each other from my other life. The life where I put on a suit every day and went to an office and talked on the phone, trying to get people to buy what I was offering, which at the time wasn't much. I had always been an astute observer of all things, people especially, and Ken and I would laugh at the stories unfolding in my newfound mysterious world of professional cooking.

Ken said, "You should write a book."

I said, "No, you should write a book. You're the writer."

"But you're the chef!"

So I wrote this book, a task that would have been impossible without Ken's help. His experience, intelligence, and the fact that we've known each other for the last twenty years didn't hurt my cause either.

I would also like to thank Graydon Carter, for his unending support of this project, and my partners and staff at the Waverly Inn for maintaining a sense of humor, and humoring me, through this painstaking, arduous, and altogether wonderful task.

I have such gratitude for my sous chefs, Domingo and Angel, who were cooking while I was typing.

I am indebted to Dan Halpern and Emily Takoudes, at Ecco/Harper-Collins. I could not have had better editors at a better publishing house. The same to my agents, Richard Abate and Becka Oliver at Endeavor, who made a pipe dream a reality, and to Karen Alinauskas for explaining the finer points of force majeure.

Special thanks to the staff at Morandi, where the bulk of this book was penned, especially Ruth, who got my coffee right every time, and Rachel, who didn't mind me spreading out on the big table before the brunch crush.

Thanks to my amazing extended family for their continuous support of my career, one that is not always kind to family life. And to Yoon, for her unending support and encouragement.

# Contents

## Author's Note

Some names, dates, places, and chronology of events have been changed or altered. I apologize to those whose stories were left on the cutting-room floor. I also apologize to those who *wish* their stories were left on the cutting-room floor.

# Introduction

When a small group of us bought The Waverly Inn in 2005, I was a relative newcomer to the hospitality trade (if you don't count thirty-five years of dining out as an editor with a liberal expense account). I may not have known a thing about how a restaurant worked, but I did know what I expected in return for my trade and 20 percent tip: convivial surroundings, gentle lighting, crisp service, and good food. The Waverly Inn—at least in my years in New York—was a stranger to all of the above. It was not without its charms, however—a compelling history being one of them. The restaurant opened its doors when Babe Ruth was still pitching for the Red Sox. It was originally billed as a tearoom, a concept that had less to do with the tastes of its proprietors and more to do with timing: the 1919 Volstead Act, ushering in Prohibition, had been passed the year before.

Set as it was in a charming little nook carved out of the ground floor of a Greenwich Village brownstone with a garden out back, The Waverly Inn survived that initial, ill-advised period of temperance and passed through many hands as the century progressed. Rumor has it that the restaurant once fronted for a brothel. Fact has it that it had been owned by the secretary to Clare Boothe, then the managing editor of

*Vanity Fair*—a coincidence I found interesting, to say the least. That she went on to marry Henry Luce, founder of *Life* and *Time* magazines (both of which I have worked for), was another point in the restaurant's favor. (As was the fact that Dawn Powell, whose 1942 novel, *A Time to Be Born*, was based on the Luce-Boothe marriage, lived across the way at 23 Bank Street.) More recently—and in relative decrepitude—the restaurant was a haunt operating in blissful disobedience of New York City's smoking ban, which, I will freely admit, further enamored me of the place.

We wanted the front room of the restaurant to have the clubby culture and warm, flattering lighting of Elaine's on the Upper East Side, or Harry's Bar, in Mayfair. And we wanted the conservatory—the garden room out back—to be warm and cheery, with a nod to San Lorenzo, in Kensington. Most important, since all the owners live in the neighborhood, we wanted The Waverly Inn & Garden (as it has officially been known) to be a local restaurant—the kind of place where the barman begins pouring your old fashioned after recognizing the pitter-patter of your footsteps as you made your way down to the door.

The little I knew about running a restaurant was matched only by my ignorance of the actual preparation of food. Aside from occasional stints in front of an outdoor grill or a campfire, I've cooked maybe a few dozen meals in my life. As a result, I have boundless admiration for anyone who can disappear into the kitchen and whip up something as simple as a ham sandwich. When it comes to restaurants, I've never been comfortable eating in places where small, precious dishes are self-consciously arranged on fragile, outsize china. I don't like foam. I don't like the solemn hush of the four-star dining room. Or having the food redescribed to me once it hits the table. Nor do I welcome the arrival of *amuse-bouches*—those little "gifts" chefs send out to make you feel special, until you look around and realize that everyone else has them too. These extras not only delay the courses you've actually ordered, but are often followed by a visit from the owner or chef.

We all sensed that The Waverly Inn had to serve food befitting its raffish history, with classic American dishes that had all but disappeared from contemporary New York menus. I looked to my favorite restaurants for influences. The original menu we drew up included the famed chili they used to serve at Chasen's, in Beverly Hills; the roast chicken from L'Ami Louis, in Paris; and the McCarthy Salad from the Bel-Air Hotel. The draft menu even included butter tarts, a Canadian delicacy (yes, you Yankee philistines, such a thing exists) that never quite caught on in the States. My mother, who is said to make the best ones in eastern Canada, was going to educate the pastry chef in the fine craft of butter tart fabrication.

Such a menu demanded a chef who could reintroduce these dishes and make them better, and healthier, than they had been before. In the movies, John DeLucie, who became not only our chef but also our partner, would play the guy who, despite all the odds, ends up with the girl. Charming, even-tempered, and wise in the ways of a true New Yorker, he is a natural chef who cooks not simply with his mind and palette but with his gut.

As you'll see in the pages ahead, John also came into the restaurant business later in life, having spent the first half as a chef-in-hiding much the way William Carlos Williams and Wallace Stevens were poets who practiced medicine and sold insurance to pay the bills. It took an early-middle-age epiphany—older readers might appreciate the feeling—to retrieve him from the business world (in his case, executive recruiting) and bring him publicly into the kitchen.

When we began sampling dishes, a number of us—investors, friends, family, and Emil Varda, our estimable manager and partner—decamped to La Bottega, the bustling Italian trattoria operated by fellow owners

Sean McPherson and Eric Goode, who were tossing drunks out of night-clubs when you were in kneesocks. By my side, in addition to my wife and kids, were two old chums. One was Brian McNally, the charming restaurateur behind The Odeon, Indochine, and 44—festive haunts that kept you in their embrace long after you should have gone home, and places that have compelled countless writers, editors, and ad men suffering from "cocktail flu" the next morning to call in sick. And there was the renowned wit Fran Lebowitz, a lay restaurant expert who likes to eat out as much as I do and is rarely shy in holding back an opinion.

Early on, we ate an extraordinary meal: beautifully prepared foie gras, bone marrow, and pork belly. It was as tasty as all get-out, but it wasn't right for our restaurant—too ornate, too fussy, suited more for Whitehall than for The Waverly. Who wants to own a restaurant where the menu *becomes* the dinner conversation? Rather than insisting on flexing his chef's muscles, John agreed, and embarked on another course.

It so happened that a few weeks later, as he was exploring The Waverly's kitchen, John unearthed a stack of old menus from the restaurant's heyday, printed on the thick, old paper stock that banks once used. The choices were simple '40s classics—steak, oysters on the half shell, chicken potpie—with barely a line of description beneath each dish. Perfecting these exact dishes, he knew, would be the key to the restaurant's success. And instead of overpowering them with fashionable culinary flourishes, he decided to restore them to perfection. (He may have gone a bit overboard on the American classic macaroni and cheese, enlivening it with white truffles and a fifty-five-dollar price tag that made the front pages of the city's esteemed tabloids. If you haven't tasted it, sell a few hundred shares of bank stock and give it a try.) While there were many contributors to the success of the restaurant, John deserves credit for envisioning a sumptuous and unpretentious menu that would lure regulars back two and sometimes three times a week in search of simple dishes that they had forgotten could be so good.

John's success in the kitchen never surprised me. What did, however, was his skill as a writer. You learn a thing or two hanging around restaurants for half your life, and John has turned that seasoned eye to himself and to this city. I remember his brand of hunger from my own days as a young man, and I know that those desperate, early days only whet the appetite for what lies ahead, and that for John DeLucie they have made his success even more delicious.

—*Graydon Carter*

# THE HUNGER

# Prologue

 It's another magical night at The Waverly Inn. Maybe it's the snow, the first dusting covering the streets of Greenwich Village during holiday season, or perhaps it's the idyllic corner location on a gorgeous Village block. All I know is that the place is electric; there's a celebrity-buzzed charge in the room, a collection of names and faces beyond anyone's wildest dreams. And here I am, chef and partner of this ridiculously hot spot with Graydon Carter, editor in chief of *Vanity Fair* magazine.

How did this happen? How did I drop everything and walk out of a go-nowhere sales career just short of my thirtieth birthday to become a chef, of all things—and then find myself here, an overnight success, seventeen years in the making? It was the kind of career trajectory that long ago I would have considered unfathomable.

Every table is full. Not just full, but crammed with bodies packed in so tightly that the waiters need Vaseline to get the plates through to the tables. And it's not your typical downtown crowd. In the corner, a mega hip-hop impresario with full entourage in tow orders yet another bottle of the vintage stuff while the waiter shaves white truffles atop his macaroni and cheese. Directly across, two of the most influential fashion designers to ever crisscross the Atlantic trade notes over dry martinis and thick juicy steaks (no fries, spinach please) on a cozy red banquette. People are smiling, laughing loudly, and conspicuously having the time of their lives. And I admit, I am, too.

Away from the glitterati buzz of the main dining room, it's 120 degrees where I stand for eight nonstop hours a night expediting from the kitchen. My cooks—Felipe, Jaciel, Adolfo, and Ramon, whose wife just gave birth to a beautiful baby boy—have other things than our celebrity clientele on their minds. Page Six is not going to be getting any scoops from these trenches.

"Chef, problem," Andre, one of my front-room waiters, barks at me in complete panic mode. "Got two lobster-both-ways at 313 and the computer says only one left."

"Who's at 313?" I ask. This is not an egalitarian operation we're running here. Rank matters. Andre mentions a very famous film director and his wife. VERY famous. Hmmmmm.

Lobster-both-ways is popular tonight. The preparation is easy enough. Take a two-pound lobster. Kill it with a sharp chef's knife straight between the eyes. Remove the claw and knuckle meat. Steam for five minutes, chop into salad with aioli, celery, and lots of shallots and chives. Chill. Reserve the tail until ordered. Paint with herb-infused oil, season with kosher salt and fresh ground pepper, grill for two or three minutes until it's just cooked through. Serve with spicy organic greens. Prepare to sell thirty. Hope famous director and wife don't order two if you are down to one.

"Well, Chef?" It's not like Andre doesn't have six four-tops to manage. I can hardly blame him for the impatient look he flashes me.

"Why don't you get some petty cash from the bar and hop a taxi to Maine," I shoot back. "I hear they have lobster there." Andre is nonplussed. He looks at me with two hands raised in a question mark.

I usually do lobster-two-ways on weeknights when there are more big spenders in the house. Serving lobster can totally mess with your food cost if you don't manage it properly. We aren't some mall-based Seafood Bonanza with twelve thermostat-controlled lobster tanks. The Waverly sits in the basement of a hundred-year-old town house. The conversion we did created a fabulous, fireplace-lined ambience complete with an original Ed Sorel mural. But when it comes to dishing out kitchen space, unless you are Alain Ducasse or one of New York's similar versions of royalty, the chef's needs are at the bottom of the list. The money guys say, "Hey, let's make a space for all of those fur coats," and the builders say, "Hey, Chef, we're taking another two hundred square feet out of your kitchen!" Half an hour later they're telling me how important it is to the bottom line that we do as many dinners as humanly possible. Bring on those lobsters!

I rifle through the stack of tickets waiting to be plated and notice there is one lobster that has not yet gone out.

"Who's at 35?" I ask Andre.

"No clue. Some bit actor who just got nominated for a Golden Globe or something." It wasn't Andre's job to give a shit about *who* we served.

"Serve both lobsters at 313," I tell him.

"But Chef, 35 already has their apps."

"Tell 'im we found mercury in the lobster tank!" Andre rolls his eyes. But I knew he'd finesse it, because Andre is good and he understands job preservation. The waitstaff would be up in arms in about two seconds. I told Felipe on the grill to fire the dinners and I let Gwen, the hostess, know that we were eighty-sixed on lobster. The director and his wife would have their dinner. Everyone else? Well. One more fire put out. All of forty-five seconds had gone by.

"Hey Chef," Gwen the hostess calls in. "There's some model asking for you at 318. I think she's on the cover of—"

"Thanks," I say, cutting her off.

"And just in case you're wondering," Gwen adds, "there is no way you can afford her."

"Appreciate the concern," I reply. I'd been at this too long to really give a shit. New York was wall to wall, and honestly, exposure to The Waverly's A-list had withered my tastes. Aren't models just people, too?

I walked through the labyrinth of tables, observing that the roasted wild striped bass was doing killer business. Note to self: order twenty more pounds of bass for the weekend. I approach 318. Arguably the most famous face (among other attributes) to grace the mailboxes of four million magazine subscribers looks up at me with recognition. It gets worse. She stands up. Was she this tall last time we met? Jesus. She flashes the most gorgeous smile I have ever seen and then she hugs me. I am caught in an embrace with one of the hottest women on the planet and all of a sudden I am speechless. It's one thing to cook for celebrities, but this is ridiculous.

When The Waverly first opened, the actor Michael Caine had lavished me with praise for my chicken potpie. Overwhelmed with gratitude and more than a little starstruck, I thanked him profusely. "Mr. Caine," I said, "no matter how bad your movies may be, I'll always go see every one." There is a reason why they keep chefs in the kitchen.

My new best friend releases me from her embrace and we share an awkward moment. I ask her how her dinner is. She grabs a pen out of her purse and scribbles something down on the white table paper that covers the tablecloths (and saves us thousands of dollars in laundry by the way). She tears off the section, leans over, and whispers something unintelligible in my ear while crumpling the paper and gently forcing it into the palm of my hand.

"Call me," she coos as I make my graceful exit. I nod, nearly taking out Andre as I head back to the kitchen. I see Lars, my tall, handsome maître d' and I quietly grab him by both collars.

"Do you have any fucking idea who's at 318?" I say, trying to tamp down my exaltation and desperation. "She just handed me her phone number. Not her agent's number. The real deal—917 and all! What the hell am I supposed to do?"

Lars, who's on the prowl for Mister Right, pats me on the cheek with his gloriously manicured fingernails. "Call her, sweetheart." And with that, he marches back onto the floor.

"I got four lobsters on 16!" Manny barks in.

"We're eighty-sixed on lobster," I bark right back.

"Great, am I supposed to read about it in the *Daily News*?" he inquires, slamming back through the door.

"Overdone New York strip on 34, coming back. Goddammit, Felipe, fire me another," I shout. Overdone steak is pure loss. Always err on the side of rare. That's first-day-of-cooking-school shit that I tell my grill guy only about forty-four times a night. He's living by a thread now.

"Graydon in the house," Lars calls in. That's my cue to make an appearance. Every night before we start rolling, Graydon puts his arms around me like some big loving teddy bear and growls, "John, did you see the reservation book? Not a good night to fuck up."

He's joking. Sort of. But he is right. He doesn't want any fuckups and neither do I. Mister Bigshot Film Director and his wife get their lobster-both-ways. The bar is three deep and Doug, my bartender, is serving up Bellini martinis to a posse of scary gorgeous women I definitely cannot afford. Four veal shanks go out, still sizzling, the smell of the garlic and butter wafting in their wake. The kitchen printer is spitting out orders like machine-gun fire and all four Viking burners are flaring like an F-16. The sweat is running down my brow and it's only eight p.m. We'll do another hundred dinners before the night is over. The place is on fire and I think: Man, I love this shit.

# Office Space

I'm late. Again. Shit. Sal is going to ream my ass out for breakfast before his first pack of cigarettes.

It is ten years before I have ever so much as cracked an egg professionally, and this is my life.

I tuck into a Zaro's cinnamon bun the size of a veal parmigiana, the *New York Times* folded under one arm, coffee in the other hand, while I make speedy tracks across the grand foyer of Grand Central, weaving through the stream of suits from the 'burbs coming to take their bite out of Manhattan. They are, I imagine, headed to glitzy offices on Park and Madison Avenues to run advertising campaigns or write magazine articles or move cocoa futures or whatever the hell it is successful people do on Park and Madison Avenues, circa 1990.

I cut into a dingy, subterranean passageway filled with the clicking of bridge-and-tunnel heels toting Century 21 bags filled with that day's lunch. The tunnel leads me to a yellowing, time-warped lobby, a throwback of an office building if ever there was one. I ride the clanking elevator in silence to the ninth floor, slip in the unpainted steel door as if to go unnoticed, only to be greeted with an accented gust by Nancy, a hardworking, efficient Irish-American girl from Queens. She informs me, in between chews of bubble gum that spray a vaguely tropical aroma into the air, that Sal is looking for me. This is never good news. Sal is the owner and founder of Brenton Financial Consultants, the company for whom I traipse uptown five days a week. My mind wanders. The Knicks are playing Boston at home. Only ten hours and twenty more minutes until tip-off.

I am an agent at a midtown Manhattan professional placement firm. We are an employment agency to the financial services industry, but not the kind that people in the high-rolling nineties are hankering to join. No, we place accountants and middle-level insurance executives. Accounting, I should point out, is the only subject in college in which I received a D. Twice. Until I landed this position, I didn't even know insurance *was* a financial industry.

My job at BFS, as it turns out, is to coax a man (and they were mostly men) from an average, decent job and place him in a far lousier one, usually for more dough, though not necessarily. Hate your boss's guts? I can fix that. Worried that the hottie in the next cubicle is going to move up the ladder faster than you? Well, she probably is. That's why I'm your guy. I'll get you that ten percent raise and add some heft to that long-term benefits package. Need an extra week for your vacation in the Poconos with the wife and kids? Here's my card. Anybody interested?

Many, in fact, are, and sometimes I get the opportunity to actually help. But truth be told, these are not my kind of guys. I have as much in common with most of them as I did with the kids who used to steal my hat in grade school and play keep-away with it. Two or three throws and I'd walk away and say "Keep the fucking hat, morons." I can't imagine it was a whole lot of fun to pick on me. It still isn't.

I walk into a cloud of smoke billowing from the open bullpen. The office is a two-room suite pocked with cheap, dented steel desks, featuring a conference room that looks to be decorated from the damaged section of the original Staples store. There are only about six of us in the firm and my direct report, Tommy, sits across from me, ostensibly teaching me the ropes. But right now all I can hear is his not-so-quiet whisper into a cupped hand over the phone saying, "Really? What are you wearing right now? Wow, what color?" He thinks he is talking quietly, all the while puffing on a Marlboro red with his giant to-go coffee ("make that three sugars and extra cream, Johnny") in the same hand as the smoldering butt. If I have to listen to another minute of this I will go nuts. Two-pack-a-day habit aside, though, Tommy is actually a good guy, and he did take me under his wing and get me off to a very quick start in the business. When I'm not gasping for oxygen, we have quite a few laughs. He looks up at me, cups the phone, and asks, "How much you pay for that piece-of-shit suit?"

"More than three payments on your new Dodge minivan," I reply. "I hear it even has power steering. Congratulations." He raises his middle finger at me and then directs it toward Sal, informing me that I'm about to have an audience with the pope. One thing about Tommy, he is always looking out for me.

Sal is pacing back and forth ignoring us, bellowing into his phone, stabbing at the air with his cigarette like a sword. The smoke cloud in the office is so thick that I'm surprised OSHA hasn't shut the place down. I slip off the jacket of my new Armani suit, a little gift to myself for a profitable last quarter. I hit my naugahyde rolling chair with a thud. Clearly one of the brain trust had been using my desk earlier that morning. I empty the overflowing ashtray and look at the list of memorandum notes impaled on a sixty-nine-cent spike—my collection of cold dead leads from which I am empowered to make my name in the world of Financial Services. Sal hangs up and leans across my desk with his beefy arms squishing together like two salamis. Who knew short-sleeved shirts were back in?

"Jones quit, kid," he announces. Ugh, I cringe. My heart sinks like a stone. Nick Jones was a really good guy in a really lousy place whom I had placed last fall. He was going through a nasty divorce, with two kids and real financial needs, and it seemed like I was doing him a favor. But a week into his new gig, he had concerns. Thirty days into it, he was unhappy. Sixty days into it, he was full-blown miserable. I told him to tough it out. Things would get better. That's what we tell everyone, since we don't earn commission unless the client lasts ninety days in their job. But this time I really thought his job would improve. Nick was a bright guy. He would figure it out. I convinced him to hang in there. He lasted ninety-one days exactly. My check would be cut at the end of the week.

Sal, of course, was nonplussed. "You did good, kid," he tells me. "You get paid. I get paid. Plus now we have a chance to get a second dip out of ol' Nicky Jones." He chuckled this maniacal laugh that sort of made me want to vault myself out the seventh-floor window as he lit another 'boro red from the one that was singeing his yellow knuckle. Sal was not about to win any Mother Teresa awards. But that's why he was the boss, the linchpin of this soulless operation. "Okay, buddy," he says. "Now get back on the phone."

I waited until Sal had finished blowing his ration of Willie Loman smoke up my ass. I knew he was trying to rally my spirits, but I had already doubled his sales volume that month. I was more concerned with maybe giving a little back on this one.

I got Nick on one ring and was greeted with stony silence. I told him we'd find him something quick. I actually had some good leads that I had personally garnered. I was now on a mission. Nick was bright and presentable, an easy placement. I assured him it was the firm, not him. I tried to make a case about the robust economy. "You'll be taking the kids to the Jersey Shore with bonus left to spare in no time," I said. He hung up on me. Shit. Too late.

I held the phone in my hand, choking on the bullpen smoke, looking out at my colleagues. Tommy was whispering again to his not-so-mysterious paramour on the phone, sipping cold coffee, lighting up another butt as if he couldn't just inhale what passed for air floating through the office. Sal was promising some hapless applicant the luxury of a nonexistent express bus from Queens that would drop him off right in front of the said new job. He would have offered a hot-air balloon if the applicant would agree to sign.

There are times in my life where I know I should have acted differently and paid attention to my instincts. Ignoring them this time was causing me pain. I'd just cost a man his livelihood and all for my lousy fee. I had responsibilities, I reasoned. I was only doing my job. I needed to make a living, too, right?

There was no escaping the pervasive sense that everything was wrong. I had tried like hell to make this latest career a good fit. For all my bitching, I liked Sal and Tommy, maybe because they were more like me than I cared to admit. Sure, I made fun of their choices—their three-for-a-hundred-dollar suits, the beers after work, the sandwiches they brought from home with inch-thick slabs of deli ham on store-bought white with mayo. "This is New York," I would lament, eating my twelve-dollar, eighteen-month-aged prosciutto panini. Deli ham and cherry Coke was just fine for them. I wanted better, as if I knew any better. Blame the world even as I floundered helpless and lost. It was a recurring problem I had, another dead-end exit on an endless highway. Except now, not only was I running out of moves, but my actions with Nick Jones had officially sanctioned me Dickhead in a Suit. A title I had richly earned. As I twirled the leads on my sixty-nine-cent post, one thing became readily apparent. It was time for a change. A very serious change.

# Happy All the Time

How had I ended up in this predicament while my friends and neighbors were riding out the cash-fat, unprecedented economic growth of the nineties?

It would be convenient to blame it on my parents, but I had not achieved the age and maturity that comes with countless years of analysis to pin it on them. Both my folks were Depression-era, working-class citizens born to Italian immigrants. My dad was a gifted musician who, for three decades, waylaid his own personal dreams of grandeur in order to feed my mom, my brother, and me by playing every wedding, bar mitzvah, and society function from the Five Towns of Long Island to Philadelphia—so that we could have a shot at making something of ourselves.

My mom worked tirelessly in an office to help make ends meet when she wasn't cooking or cleaning, which, to the best of my recollection, was rarely. She was the disciplinarian, and any time me or my younger brother would get out of line or answer her back we would get our asses whacked with the massive wooden spoon she used to delicately stir the marinara sauce she served at family dinner on Sunday afternoons. The mere sound of the drawer rattling as she reached for the spoon was enough to evoke terror. Of course my grandmother was always there to coddle and nurture us with a bowl of pastina, or spaghetti with butter, or a remarkable soup she would whip up with the most delicate chicken meatballs ever. Food was our panacea and a constant presence woven into every celebration. Someone was born, let's eat. First communion, more food. High school graduation, a wedding, bring on the feast. Even death could be grieved a little more comfortably with a nice spread of antipasti and, of course, the company of an extraordinarily loving family.

Growing up, there was no legacy of academic success for me to aspire to. No family business or trust to inherit. Just two loving parents who wanted the very best for their kids. I started working weekends with my dad when I was around fourteen years old. I'd carry the speakers, amps, and sound system for the band, and haul my dad's giant Fender Rhodes piano into the hall. I would set up the equipment, then connect all the wires and microphones, make sure it all worked, and then change into a tuxedo and cruise the bar mitzvah or wedding for girls. Pick your religious ceremony. I was completely agnostic in my tastes. It was like going to a free party every weekend. I wonder if my dad ever realized why I'd ask him for the car keys in the middle of the opening E flat major seventh chord of "Misty." I'd get back to the party with the bar mitzvah boy's sister in time to light a candle for the ceremony, the back of her dress undone.

By seventeen, I started playing and singing with the band myself. I could perform "Hava Nagila," "Always & Forever," and the requisite Kool and the Gang's "Celebration." After we'd sung the closing notes of the *Fiddler on the Roof* medley, I'd break it all down and we'd head for the Long Island Expressway, my dad humming along to jazz on late-night radio behind the wheel of his '74 Buick Estate wagon. Once home, we'd unload the wagon and, bleary-eyed, I'd head up to bed. My father, still pumped on adrenaline from performing, would make himself some tea with crackers and jam and put a record on his vintage Marantz stereo and listen until the wee hours, or until my mother woke up and screamed for him to come to bed.

As a result of my dad's professional calling and the thousand bat and bar mitzvahs I had played, I developed a love and appreciation for the Jews. They were as crazy as we were. Family-oriented, emotional, dramatic, loving, and passionate like Italians. And the food. We lived for kasha, kasha varnishkes, sweetbreads, smoked sable, lox and onions. We actually started having kosher food one night a week at home. My dad would stop at Ben's Deli, near where he taught piano, and bring us kugel, the best bagels, and chopped liver, which we hated but he would make us eat any way. Blintzes, rice pudding—you name it. We were nuts about food.

I attended a couple of years of local community college before enrolling at NYU for business and, I admit, for its proximity to the downtown scene more than for any great professional aspirations. What I lacked in educational drive I more than compensated for in creative desire. I played guitar all throughout high school, and there was little doubt that I had inherited my dad's music gene. He was born with golden ears and could listen to a tune once and have it down instantly. If it was a particularly difficult melody with a lot of sharps and flats, then two listens, at the most. He must have known a thousand songs by heart and could play them all in every conceivable key. As much as I admired him, his skill was a tough thing to live up to.

Maybe that's why I grew up so scared to pursue anything I actually enjoyed. I loved basketball as a kid and spent all the hours allotted by Dad for piano practice shooting foul shots. Sports were *not* his thing, and he did everything he could to discourage my brother, Eugene, and me from participating. He saw no value in it whatsoever, and why would he? He didn't need the escape from his nine-to-five that other fathers did when they coached or cheered at games. My dad was already doing exactly what he wanted. He pulled me aside one day, leaned down on one knee, and said very softly and reasonably, "Suppose you got so good at basketball that every time you shot the ball it went in? Whadaya got? *Nothing!* Now, on the other hand, imagine you can play a beautiful song. You could make yourself and a lot of other people very happy." It was a compelling argument, all but lost on a stubborn twelve-year-old who liked to shoot foul shots.

I took the first job I could find out of college, which happened to be selling ads for a direct-marketing newsletter. This, I can say with great confidence, was the first step on a very unsexy and miserable career path. My twenties, professionally speaking, were an indistinct series of lows, a one-dimensional plane of career dissatisfaction. It seemed like every three months I found myself reviewing my choices for the ump-teenth time. I hated midtown, hated putting on a suit every day, and hated the smoke-streaked walls at BFC. More time than I care to admit was spent idly noodling on my guitar, passively contemplating a music and songwriting career, while my beloved Knicks wallowed again in mediocrity.

I'm sure I wasn't the only guy parading up and down the streets of Manhattan without a clue what to do with his life. The subways were full of bleary-eyed drones plugged into their bulky Sony Walkmans, the *New York Post* opened to the sports page, ricocheting from home to work and back again five times a week. The only thing that separated me from the masses was a slightly spoiled attitude and a probable case of undiagnosed ADD. I knew I had to get off the executive recruiting dead-end track. Dragging these poor insurance guys from one lousy job into another while I reaped the blood money was unsettling. I had such contempt for them and was jealous of them simultaneously. I just didn't know where the next stop was.

Several years earlier, I had somehow talked my way into a job as director of advertising sales at a consumer magazine start-up. It was unlikely anyone so unqualified would be handed a position that far up the totem pole. The whole operation was undercapitalized with a trendy highbrow concept that was suspect at best. Probably every remotely qualified candidate had balked, but now I was their man. The prospect of breaking into the glamorous world of big-brand blue-chip names was alluring. Isn't this what I was supposed to want? My slice of the good life? I sold one ad in nine months because the media buyer had a crush on me. Or more likely because she had a few extra grand in her multi-million-dollar budget and took pity on an earnest soul. As fate would have it, the ad was printed incorrectly. How embarrassing for me and for her. Next.

Time seemed to be running out. And in reality it was. I was nearly thirty years old. My friends were all married, buying homes, and starting to have kids. I was living with my long-time girlfriend, Gina, a gifted stylist who worked at a top salon in SoHo. I was even wrestling with a decision as obvious as tying the knot. I was still very much a kid, with a patchy goatee, big commitment issues, a healthy sense of foreboding, and a very short attention span.

There was one path that I had never seriously considered but that actually raised my spirits—even without the third espresso of the morning. I still played my electric guitar seven days a week, sometimes late into the night. So how about music? My dad put two kids through college with his music. Maybe this was an option that needed to be explored. I wasn't so sure about the starving artist thing, but I thought what the hell and decided to see if I couldn't pull a band together. It didn't have to be a career. Just some guys gigging.

I ran an ad in the *Village Voice* and the response was instantaneous. I liked the first guy who answered. He was a keyboard player and he dug all the same musicians as me—Stevie Wonder, Luther Vandross, all the seventies horn bands like Earth, Wind & Fire and The Ohio Players. We talked concerts, harmony, chord changes, and funk. Great, I thought, this is the stuff that lights me up. Then he excused himself and disappeared into the bathroom for a half hour. My keyboardist-to-be finally emerged, pupils dilated, and seemingly residing now in an alternative universe. I escorted him to the door.

The next guy to respond was a singer. His name was Tyrone, and he brought along his "boy," Tiki, whose role in the potential band was as yet undetermined. Tyrone sanded wood floors during the day, and I noticed him eyeballing the satin finish on my floors. We were actually getting along pretty well, and he sang a few bars and sounded great. This is going well, I thought, until I slipped out to the bathroom and returned to find a huge shiny black handgun on my kitchen table. "Is that a thirty-eight or a nine?" I asked casually, trying to sound street-smart or at the very least not piss my pants. Tyrone and Tiki could barely contain themselves, they were laughing so hard. After they composed themselves, I found out that Tiki had just landed a job as a New York City corrections officer and wanted to show off his new piece. I realized that I was going to have to change my taste in music or find a different way of making new friends.

My foray into the music world was on life support when a friend of a friend introduced me to a young music student and singer named Joy. Life is full of pivotal moments and I had a sinking feeling this was one of them. Joy was pretty and petite with coffee-colored skin, and she was blessed with an extraordinary voice, and perfect pitch to boot. It didn't hurt that we struck it off like long-lost friends.

We booked some recording time in an old run-down studio in the West 40s and started putting together a demo. I found myself writing like someone had hoisted a lead weight from my back, and Joy sang my lyrics with incredible soul, never wavering out of key.

Joy was much more driven and optimistic, not to mention talented, than I was. She was going to make music a legitimate career at any cost, and she got us booked into a Thursday-night gig as the lead act to a band that was getting some notoriety. One night I was in the Green Room, which served as the coatroom in the winter, warming up when this other band's guitar player asked to borrow my tuner. "No problem, bro," I said. Guitar players are notoriously competitive. Still, I plugged him in.

The guy looked familiar and finally I asked, "Do I know you?"

"Elliott," he offers, barely looking up.

"Elliott Randall?" I say, trying desperately not to look blown away.

"Yeah, that's me," he replies. Elliott Randall played the lead guitar solo in Steely Dan's hit song "Reelin' in the Years." Arguably one of the best rock 'n' roll guitar solos ever. I was about to play on the same stage as the guy who played that lead.

This was not small shit for me, and it was a much-needed antidote to my day job. But then fate threw a curveball. Joy's wispy, sexy sultry voice landed her a three-month gig touring Japan. She asked me to go as her guitar player. I was faced with a real crisis here. Three months holed up in Osaka with my guitar and Joy with that incredible cocoa complexion, or continue on my inexorable 6th Avenue local commute to BFS. Gina, in her own inimitable style, solved the dilemma. "Do what you want. Go to Japan. I'm sure you'll have no problem paying the rent on this apartment—alone!—when you get back unemployed."

I returned my glossy copy of Frommer's *Japan*, dug my suit out of the trash, and left for work in the morning.

# Ingredients

The situation at BFS was reaching critical mass. Sal was looking for an up-tic in production from everyone, which was hardly the morale boost this office needed. What's more, despite the fact that Joy had abandoned me for her shot at stardom in Japan, I had not lost my jones for playing. So the miles of speaker wire, guitar cords, broken strings, and effects boxes remained strewn all over the apartment like a bomb detonated at one of those music stores on West 48th Street. Gina was starting to lose her patience with me. It could have been the mess. Or perhaps it was the listless funk I had settled into, staring at late-night reruns and bemoaning the day I was born. I was a bit prone to the dark side, and she was definitely growing weary of it. And who could blame her?

One evening when she was out, no doubt getting some blessed relief from my languor, I invited my brother and a couple of our buddies over to watch the Knicks take on the Heat. As I watched from our closet-sized kitchen, I absentmindedly whipped up a homemade marinara with spaghetti and a little parmigiano Reggiano. It was the recipe I had watched my grandmother and then my mom make over and over. I tended to cook as happily and casually at home as other people sat down to do a crossword. It was one of my true sources of relaxation, and I did it all the time. A little company, all the better. I handed the warm bowls of pasta to the cast of slackers on my long leather couch. The sounds of men talking faded to the slurping of spaghetti and sauce.

I will admit, the smell of the garlic drifting through the apartment, the satisfying sight of my friends happy in a row sucking down dinner, and the odd sense of peace that floated over me even as the final buzzer sounded was inspiring. I loved the vibe of making people happy. It was like my father playing them a song. This was one thing I could do. Maybe? I could cook. I've always loved food and everything related to it. My mother, my aunts, my grandmother from Bari, Italy—they were all great cooks, and I had inherited at least some of that DNA, as a rank amateur, of course. But this was a comfort zone, I realized. And how gratifying it was.

I didn't know the first thing about the cooking business. But that evening, for the first time, I gave thought to whether I really was going to seek out something entirely different—or was it just another night, another Knicks loss, and another all-too-brief respite en route to one more dreary day on the job?

I decided to take matters into my own hands and call a guy I vaguely knew named Andrew. He was the son of my dad's lifelong friend and he happened to be chef at a fancy and wildly popular East Side restaurant, Sign of the Dove—a place where my family never ate and where I had never set foot. We all knew it was special. One of those places you talked about and equated with wealthy people or society dinners that made the evening news. My parents were always talking about Andrew. And he was much acclaimed when I was growing up. I hadn't thought about him in years. If ever there were a time to call in a favor, this seemed like it.

While I have a tendency to wallow in the moment, conversely I am also very good in crisis. So sometimes I create one to motivate. In the case of my unhappy job situation, I was doing a bang-up job. So I got Andrew on the phone and explained that I was thinking about changing careers. "You probably don't remember me," I said, "but I'm thinking about going into food. I'd maybe like to become a chef." And he says something like, "You're too old, it's a miserable job, don't do it." And I think, "Great, where do I start?"

Once I get an idea in my head, no matter how irrational, I'm actually pretty good at executing. And all of a sudden this is feeling like a really good idea. The thought of schlepping stockpots instead of cold-calling dead leads sounded exhilarating. It seemed active and real. Everything about my current life was not. I wanted to get my hands dirty. The question was where and how.

I called every school I could think of—Culinary Institute of America, the French Culinary Institute, Peter Kump—all the well-known places where the skilled and gifted chefs got educated. I got all the colorful brochures, with the handsome, immaculate-looking guys whisking away in their bright white toques. What I learned was that the price tag was prohibitive. At the bottom of my stack, I'd stuffed a New School catalog, the latest copy fresh from the free sidewalk stand next to the porn newspapers and community news. I thumbed through the catalog until I located a class called Master Chefs Course. The fee might have been fifteen hundred bucks, if that, for twelve weeks, a fraction of the cost of the other courses. Now, for a relatively small investment, I could figure out if this dream had legs or if, like so many of my other schemes, it would go up in smoke. There wasn't a lot to lose and yet I had this sense that there was everything to lose. My mother, of all people, happened to call at that moment, so, emboldened, I told her I was quitting my job to pursue a career as a chef. With all the honesty and candor only a mother can muster, she screams across the entire length of Long Island, "ARE YOU NUTS?"

A week later, with Gina's support—and the powers vested in me by the New York State Department of Unemployment Insurance—I found myself walking three steps down below ground level into the door of a renovated brownstone in Greenwich Village. I entered a wide-open converted kitchen space lined with Viking stoves, steel pot racks, industrial-size butcher blocks, and four huge refrigerator-freezers. I found myself face-to-face with a madcap cast of characters: housewives, hobbyists, actresses, would-be caterers, weekend entertainers, singles looking for soul mates, soul mates looking for distraction, and even a professional cook looking to hone her skills. There was one other guy in the class, a successful business type, it seemed, as evidenced by his expensive Italian leather shoes. I had the impression he was either slumming between stints trading companies or just plain bored out of his head.

The instructor, Carrie, was a thirty-something, driven, caring, and detail-oriented teacher and ex–restaurant chef. She struck me as someone who would take no bullshit in her kitchen—or her life for that matter. The problem was, I had a long history of bullshitting my way through most everything. I am not proud of this trait, but you go with what works. In the long view, it did not serve me well. Fortunately, no one can bullshit their way through thirty quarts of veal stock.

Under Carrie's watchful eye, the twelve of us sautéed and chopped and cleaned and scraped and blanched and roasted and limped our way into some semblance of utility in her kitchen. Her class may have provided little more than a way to pass the time for the bulk of the student body, but she wasn't going to let any of us out of there without at least some decent skills. We met five times a week, and all of a sudden I found myself looking forward to those hours with a passion I hardly recognized. Not only had my mood improved, but I found myself hitting every specialty market in town, dragging home grocery sacks full of fresh breads and buffalo mozzarella and local herbs, organic greens, glorious cuts of meat and delicate fish fillets from shops I had never set foot in before. A whole new world was emerging. I was cooking in the mornings and cooking in the evenings and something was changing in me. For the first time in my life, I felt like I had found an aptitude. I bought *Larousse Gastronomique* and read it cover to cover. I scoured The Strand and Kitchen Arts & Letters for obscure cookbooks and read *Gourmet* and the *Times* Wednesday food section religiously. I was becoming thoroughly obsessed and falling in love all at the same time.

But still my old attitude problem would crop up occasionally. One morning I was dicing carrots for a soup and I was doing a half-assed job because I figured I could, all the while flirting with a sexy bored housewife just to get a smile. Carrie worked her way down the butcher block line until she got to me and sized up my handiwork. She had painstakingly explained to us the necessity and technique of dicing these vegetables into one-quarter-inch by one-quarter-inch squares. Anything short of that would get you fired from your first job. That was the reality she was prepping us for. She took one look at my carrots, picked up the board, and dumped the whole lot into the garbage. I stared at her with a hopeful shrug. She told me to stop batting my brown lashes at her, do it right or get the hell out!

Life deals you the oddest lessons at times. The key is knowing when to pay attention. I don't know why this perfectly lovely woman running a cooking class in a brownstone should have cared a rat's ass about me, but her words cut like a paring knife. I was truly ashamed and, most importantly, I realized I had something at stake. I did not want to phantom my way through this, too. BFS was a mere four stops north on the subway.

Two weeks later, as part of a class demonstration, all twelve of us had to cook a chicken cutlet. I had watched my grandmother and my mom do this a thousand times and figured that by this stage of the class most anyone could do it in their sleep. In no time the kitchen was sizzling with the sound of hot butter and oil, and we cooked and plated a dozen cutlets and waited as Carrie walked the line. You could feel the tension as we all stood with our arms stiffly by our sides, peeking over at one another's work. Some came out smoky and dark because the pan was too hot. Others came out unappetizingly pale and rubbery because the pan wasn't hot enough. The one that stood out the most was the cutlet cooked by Wall Street guy. Somehow, remarkably, his one lonely chicken cutlet came out with a ragged hole right through the center.

I remember the way mine looked—the skin brown and beautiful and perfectly caramelized. It was chicken cutlet art, the way I remember my grandmother's looked on her kitchen table.

We had a silly, formal graduation ceremony. Some of my class-mates brought their kids. Wall Street guy brought his girlfriend, who looked like she had just stepped off the boat from South Beach. I came alone, since Gina had five hair appointments scheduled for that day and, frankly, we weren't in any position to give up those tips. Carrie made presentations to the whole class; she took it seriously and made us all appreciate what we had learned and what we might face if we ever hefted a twelve-inch cleaver by choice again. At the end of her remarks she announced the Student Most Likely to Succeed.

I was as embarrassed as I was mortified to hear my name called, and yet at the same time I had a catharsis. I would never play the guitar as well as I or my dad had hoped. I was not going to become the lawyer that my mom had longed for, thank God. But even at this novice stage—a thirty-year-old man contemplating a young person's career—I recog-nized that Carrie had taught me something that no top-drawer cooking class ever could. I had bullshitted my way through far too many years at far too many things that I did not care about, and it had gotten me no-where. In that brownstone basement kitchen, all that changed. I learned that I could be honest with myself, consequences be damned. It is a les-son I have never forgotten.

One week later I found myself working as a professional cook in the subbasement kitchen of Dean & DeLuca Gourmet.

# Was It Him?

It's a quiet rainy Monday night in the city, the kind of night when you order in and hunker down with a book. Not for us, though. The Waverly Inn is hopping. We've got all four fireplaces burning and we're flat out of tables by 8:30—one after another, gone, as unexpected VIPs show up needing a cozy banquette to hold court. Table for four? Not so fast. The Princess of Jordan has arrived unannounced with some hungry royal friends. It will only take her security detail a few minutes to make sure the place is "secure." I'm surprised she did not arrive by armored car. The diamonds around her neck and in her ears would bankrupt a country of considerable size. We let security do their thing.

Meanwhile, Gwen, our exotically pretty, overeducated hostess, who can seat people in at least four languages, has three men in fancy dark straight-leg suits standing impatiently, awaiting what they expect will be a star seating. She's glowering at Emil, our general manager and my partner in day-to-day crime. Emil is a handsome and winsome self-proclaimed European refugee whose deft administration of the Waverly door policy has already become legend. He has refrained from seating the dashing trio because they are down in the reservation book for a party of four, and as is the case in most fine restaurants, we do not seat incomplete parties. Unless, of course, said party is Bill and Hillary, for example, and Chelsea is running late, jammed up on the number one downtown local.

"What's the problem?" I ask, stepping between Gwen and Emil.

"I'm trying to seat these guests at table 701," Gwen implores, "but Emil says no." Note: 217 is arguably the worst table in the entire restaurant. Every place has one—close to the kitchen door where you can hear and smell everything. If you're one of those people who'd rather not know what goes on behind the scenes with your meal, stay away from 217. Even worse if your mastery of Spanish is ninth-grade level or beyond, because you are so close to the action, you might hear some things not normally associated with fine dining. Far be it from me, however, to step on Emil's toes. He doesn't tell me how to cook (not on a regular basis) and I don't tell him how to keep peace in our precious front-of-the-house real estate. Still, *no one* wants to be seated there.

Gwen leans in close to me, whispering, "The guy in the beard? I saw him on Letterman last night. He's a hot new comedian."

Great. I roll my eyes, mixing a cocktail in my head of two parts sarcasm, one part cynicism, and a jigger of is this really happening? Everyone here is somebody. Emil, who has overheard Gwen's comment, cuts in, his voice rising an octave in that enchanting European accent, its precise provenance undetectable to the untrained ear. "I do not give shit about silly American comedy man." With that he walks away, his point made. It's his game. They're going to wait.

Fifteen minutes later, I can only assume that the fourth member of Silly American Comedy Man's party has arrived, because the dupe from the kitchen printer begins to click, click, click for table 217. A dupe is the duplicate check that spits out of the kitchen printer and tells me what you have ordered and how you want it cooked. I keep a running tab all night long on who's ordering what, what is going where, and what if anything is selling at a rapid clip. It's the only way to manage the insanity going on in the kitchen. Dupes rarely create more than the tiniest mental static for me. This one, however, is a foot long and still printing. Table 217 has ordered practically everything on the menu. The tuna tartare, the country salad with Berkshire lardons, the beets with the Humboldt Fog goat's cheese—the beets were roasted earlier in the day with a little cinnamon stick, coriander, star anise, herbs, and a whole head of garlic thrown in. They are tender and have the right amount of bite, tasting like rich sweet earth, and they've been going like mad. The dupe keeps firing: artichoke, the crab cakes with Old Bay aioli, the grilled baby octopus. Christ, this is a ton of food for Silly American Comedy Man and his thin, seemingly fit friends whom I saw out front ten minutes ago. They certainly didn't look famished. What now? The chicken liver—get those sourdough toast points working. Short ribs, chicken, pork chop. "Hey, Papi," I say, using the term of endearment that I use a hundred times a night for my Latin American staff, "those oysters are miniature. *Mas grande ahora!*" Four slender guys out to dinner in the West Village would never order that much food. That can only mean one thing: reviewer in the house!

Here in New York City at Graydon Carter's new dining Mecca, we have become a target, with a big fat bull's-eye on the back of my chef's coat. The place has been all over the press, but the ink has hardly been about the food. It's been mostly about who comes to eat here, who owns the place, who threw a drink in which famous ex's face, and other barely true if not downright fabricated tales. The presence of celebrity, I am fast learning, is tasty bait to the food press. Everyone is gunning for us and I'm getting used to ducking. However, there is one food scribe—one arbiter of taste who matters, personally and professionally, and that is Frank Bruni of the *New York Times*. SHIT. I am praying. Please not at table 701.

I've personally never laid eyes on the guy. Could one of those guests we kept waiting have been him? I keep a grainy Internet photo pasted above my station in the kitchen, in the office above the fax machine, and on the employee bathroom wall next to the mirror above the sink, lest a staff member spot him first. I peer out the door at 701. None of these dudes look like my dog-eared photo. But then again, it's the Web. My photo could be circa 1984. I need another opinion, and fast.

I slip out of the kitchen and nearly get bowled over by a food runner. Dodging him, I accidentally bump my hip into one of the customers wedged into 217, squeezed between the barely adequate four-top and the kitchen door. The party of four that is now looking a lot like Frank Bruni and guests glares at this uninvited interruption. I apologize and sidle over to the bar to elicit Doug's expertise, because I know he once worked at a Bruni-reviewed joint.

"Got a second?" I call out over the crowd three-deep at the bar.

Doug is pouring four shaken gin martinis, the tiniest shaven bits of ice glimmering on the surface of the drink. The guy is an artist who concocts a hundred liquid masterpieces a night. He has no time for me or anyone else at this moment. Still.

"Bruni at 217?" I ask, cutting to the chase.

Doug gets it. We all do. He squeezes out from behind the bar, leaving about forty-five drinks unmade. He makes a quick beeline to check out the dashing quartet at the tiny table, with me close on his trail.

"Hmmm," Doug says. "Blue eyes, kind of handsome. Could be. Hard to tell." Just then another food runner staggers out of the kitchen, arms loaded with heavy plates—my handiwork—and inadvertently slams his hip into the back of the fourth jammed-in chair of 701 with a vengeance. Again! These poor bastards are getting hammered. My heart drops. Emil joins us, as always alert to anything that goes on in the dining room. We're about as subtle as the Three Stooges. Surely Emil knows what Frank Bruni looks like. I ask, but he nods me off with a surly "Zat ees *certainly* not him." And about two seconds later, "Ees it?"

I steal one last surreptitious glance at 701. Possible Frank Bruni is exploring his plate of tuna tartare with a fork as if searching for parasites. He glances up at me and flashes a wordless slash of a smile before taking a bite—a bite that will determine whether all I've worked for is worthy of the most happening stage in New York. My stomach flip-flops as I walk back into the kitchen. The printer is spitting out orders and the hot line is running like a '72 Oldsmobile 442. I've done what I can do. Bruni's a customer like anyone else. At this point it is out of my control. Whatever else happens, there is a room full of people having a splendid time and enjoying their meal right now. I'm not kidding myself— career-wise that is not enough. You can't put a price on a rave review. On the other hand, based on the chattering congenial buzz just out of range from my post and the empty plates being bussed in by the armful, we're at least doing something half right.

# Trial by Salad

Gina and I were married on a sultry August Sunday afternoon at Our Lady of Pompeii, a towering cathedral on Carmine Street, overlooking Father Demo Square off of 6th Avenue in Greenwich Village. Following the ceremony, we left the church in the back of a white-horse-drawn carriage, followed by 130 of our closest friends and family en route to an elegant Bedford Street town house a few blocks away for the reception. The only thing more palpable than the ominous humidity and the promise of a thunderstorm was the sheer look of terror on my mother's face, petrified not about our future together but whether there would be enough food to feed everyone at the reception. "Why can't you get married on Long Island where your cousin got married?" she moaned. "They have such nice veal. And where is everyone going to park?"

Our romance had begun in suburban Long Island, where we both were cut from a very different cloth than our fellow Camaro-driving, big-hair, rocking classmates and neighbors. We lived across the street from each other and attended the same school. Gina was petite, edgy, and very cute, the grooviest girl I had ever met—and thoroughly unobtainable for a guy like me. I knew as much about dating as I did about cooking back in those unendurable high school days. She dated dangerous unsavory types, the kind of guys who didn't even know my social circle of band musician friends even existed. I was resigned to the fact that we would be friends and nothing more. But we were drawn into a fast friendship over our musical tastes, favoring R&B and soul over Pat Benatar and Journey. We embraced the disco craze and would sneak off to the city to dance in the clubs. She would get in with her friends. I would wait for hours in front of the velvet ropes. But once in, the music, the people, the life was intoxicating. We were seduced by the dazzling urban life while living in a very dull suburban environment. After we had both exhausted lengthy college relationships, we fell completely into sync. We never looked back.

On the first day of my new cooking career, Gina actually got out of bed and made a pot of coffee at six in the morning as I got ready to commute to day one at Dean & DeLuca. We had moved to Carroll Gardens, a Brooklyn outpost back then and the neighborhood I was born in. We were basically broke. Gina was cutting at a trendy salon in SoHo and doing okay. I had been through so many jobs that economy of rent seemed about the only stable move we could make. We eventually hoped to buy back in downtown Manhattan, but for now my uncle Vinny had one of those old tenement buildings and an apartment was available. Suffice it to say my mom made sure we got the "family" deal. It was a railroad apartment with wooden floors so warped you could roll a melon from the back end to the front without giving it a push. We had painted the place in loud primary colors, covered every square inch in food art, and hung pots and pans we had scored on a trip to Europe. Of course, no friends would venture out to what they considered the Wild West that was Brooklyn back in those days, but we were happy.

I hopped a city-bound F train at the ungodly hour of 6:30 a.m. The train dropped me off promptly at 7:00 right in front of Dean & DeLuca on Broadway just below Houston Street, the gateway to SoHo. New York has always been known for its specialty foods, but Dean & DeLuca was one of the first to put it out there for the wider public. The celebrated specialty food emporium was legend for its vast array of marvelously presented epicurean delights.

I had landed this job in a fashion completely uncharacteristic of me, at least the me who had previously hunted jobs through the *New York Times* classifieds. As cooking school had drawn to an end, I had walked into Dean & DeLuca one morning on a whim, fought my way through the throngs of attractive patrons in search of rare caviar or truffles or perhaps some beautiful blood oranges just in from Sicily.

I tracked down the general manager, who turned out to be a slight fellow, gray at the temples, with the facial expression of a deer in headlights. I proudly announced my new cooking pedigree and asked if he had a job. As it turned out, there was a real shortage of cooks in New York at the time. He gave me a look that said, "Please somebody fucking work here!"—and hired me on the spot.

A week later, I entered the store in my Calvin Klein jeans, black turtleneck, and Doc Martins, toting a messenger bag and looking for where a new hire might report. I wandered through the aisles, drinking in the rows of gleaming vegetables, fruit, coffees, teas, oils, spices, and condiments. There were brilliantly displayed bowls and plates and cookware, and row after row of dish towels, knives, pepper mills, graters, colanders, mandolines, and implements I had never even laid eyes on. The meat counter was stacked with cuts of beef splayed like doorstops, and the fish counter was glistening with ice covering an assortment of seafood that reminded me of the morning markets in Italy. The fish guy, in boots and a bloody white coat, was laying out a display of splendid bright-orange wild Alaskan salmon. I asked him where I might find Louise, the woman to whom I was to report to in the prep kitchen. He pointed to a double-swinging metallic door at the rear of the store. I pushed my way through and descended a steep flight of stairs into the dimly lit basement.

Imagine entering a submarine and you'll get the gist. The place was crudely painted in battleship gray and filled with rows of stainless-steel tables. Industrial stoves lined the walls, and they were already aflame with stockpots and steamers and kettles and fry pans the size of a table-top, manned by grill chefs shaking and stirring and tossing in the flickering light of the flames. There were probably a half dozen prep cooks at work, washing and dicing, chopping and loading containers full of vegetables. I stood in the midst of this beehive of activity feeling lost, bordering on panic. I fought back the sinking feeling that I had made a terrible mistake and finally tracked down Louise. She turned out to be a young, high-strung Indian woman in a stained chef's coat and baker's hat. She gave me exactly four seconds to offer my spiel before she handed me a soiled recipe for red bliss potato salad, planted me in front of a cutting board, and said, "Make this."

Like any first day on the job, there was a drowning sense of complete unfamiliarity, but there was nowhere to run and hide. I asked Louise where to dump my stuff and she pointed to a closet where I also found clean cook's whites and an apron. I returned to the prep table where I had been assigned. Louise was gone. I was on my own. A heaping mound of red bliss potatoes had already been surgically sliced into one-eighths. I loaded them into a steel bowl as large as a wading pool and started adding the ingredients that the recipe called for: scallions, chopped bacon, shallots, vinegar, scoops of kosher salt and ground pepper, and heart-stopping gobs of Hellmann's mayonnaise that I scooped out of a gallon jug. I gingerly folded the ingredients in my bowl with a rubber spatula, getting into a rhythm. This was the real deal. It looked delicious, and since the first thing you are taught is to always taste your food, I plucked out a slice of mayonnaise-y red bliss potato and tasted it. One bite and I nearly broke off a tooth! Mr. Professional No-More-Working-Stiff-Corporate-Guy, chef-in-the-making neglected to realize that the potatoes had not been cooked. Day one and I was proud owner of twenty-five pounds of ruined, uncooked potato salad.

Mortified, I looked around the kitchen hoping that the world's largest in-sinkerator would appear and allow me to rid myself of this awful mistake. Instead, Louise appeared. She said, "Let me taste that" and before I could stop her, she had a bite of spud in her mouth. She spit it across the table and shouted, "These aren't cooked."

"I know," I said, trying desperately to think of some excuse to explain this disaster. Nothing came to mind.

"Jesus Christ, I can get fired for this," she announced, checking the coast behind her. *She* could get fired? I thought. What about me? "Fuck, just make it again!"

Somehow I survived day one. And two, and three. By the end of the first week even the subway didn't look so bad in the gray early mist of dawn. For the next four weeks I made potato salad, Caesar salad, pasta salad, egg salad, deviled eggs, couscous, hummus, tahini, three-bean salad, shrimp salad, crab salad—you name it—anything that could take mayonnaise, extra-virgin, or any other fat molecules to hold it together and give it taste. I prepared London broil and oregano chicken, pork roast, lamb roast, veal roast. Salt and apply heat. Perfect. I worked the sandwich line and created masterpieces of Genoa salami and prosciutto, cappicola, mortadella, mozzarella, speck, bresaola, and Parma ham. I served them up on focaccia, baguettes, boules, ficelles—all brought in daily from the best bakeries the city had to offer.

I was not miserable during this trial by fire. There was something primal about being elbows-deep in all this produce and animal flesh, day in and day out six days a week. But oddly enough, I was not learning a lot. There was an assembly-line mentality to the place. The cooks who worked in the prep basement were not aspiring chefs for the most part. They were decent hardworking men and women who were flying low under the radar for any number of reasons savory and otherwise, making a decent wage to feed a family. I had gained a deep respect for these people who worked so hard and without complaint, but I was looking for more culinary inspiration. I ended up getting it from a cook whose name I can't recall and, quite likely, may never have known. But he knew mine. "Hey, dickhead, come over here and taste this!"

To the best of my recollection, I had never met an ex-con before. But my first guru in the cooking life looked like the bad guy out of an animated cartoon. He had long, luxurious hair tucked under the most puffy cotton toque, and prison tattoos lining his arms. He was tall and lean with wild eyes that weren't always focused. I steered clear of him when he was working with knives, because there was no telling what he might cut off, deliberately or otherwise. He cooked with a manic intensity, like a rogue jazz player, by ear. I guess he saw something in me, because we coexisted with this unspoken understanding that cooking was better than other things we might be doing. Certainly what *he* might be doing.

One morning he tasted a soup of mine that I was working on. He burst into laughter, all crazy and out of context, and dragged me to his station. He told me to shut up and pay attention, as he sharpened a twelve-inch, beat-up Wusthof like he was preparing for an execution. I shut up all right, and I watched as he chopped with complete abandon: pounds of tomato, onion, leeks, zucchini, carrots, bunches of basil—and loaded it all into a simmering stockpot full of white, green, and kidney beans. He salted and peppered to taste with mannerisms that suggested the delicacy of a surgeon more than the meaty paws of a con. Finally, he stuck my nose in the stockpot and handed me a metal spoon. With my face deep in the steaming, simmering cauldron, I took a spoonful and, braving third-degree burns, sampled.

It might have been the best goddamned soup I ever tasted up to that point, rich and balanced and complex. When I told him, he ignored me and walked away and started dismembering chickens for a stock. I sensed that he was secretly pleased, for about a millisecond. Then he started cursing at me for standing still for so long and put me to work on a mound of turnips and rutabagas. This guy, whoever he was and from whatever fucked-up insane background he emerged, knew how to cook. And as I stood there contentedly chopping twenty pounds of root vegetables, I thought, I want to cook like *that*.

# Crossing Bloomingdale's

It didn't take long for my old demons to come back and haunt me. You can decide to turn your life entirely upside down, but that doesn't guarantee instant gratification. A few weeks into Dean & DeLuca and I was restless. Sure, I was surrounded by all this great food, but it was hardly the glamorous life. I was spending my days doing my best to make conversation with non-English-speaking immigrants and hanging out with bored-out-of-their-skull prep cooks and ex-cons and people on the lam from who knows what, cooking for a living before they made their next move. Not that I was sitting in judgment. I was kind of digging it, in fact. It was a relief after two years at BFC listening to insurance executives and accountants bitch about their perceived ills. My new work environment revealed a slice of life that suburbia and white-collar New York had never afforded me. My new work friends had real problems. Jorge, a speedy little guy with an aerodynamic hairstyle, had a wife and two kids in the old country, a girlfriend and a young child here, and after a number of tequilas one night at the local hangout, it seems, a new boyfriend.

Jake, one of our cooks, was a formerly successful screenwriter in full nervous breakdown recovery mode. Not so long ago he was at the top of his game, and now he's dishing out truffled egg salad from behind the prepared-foods counter. I could picture him wrapping his arms around the Academy Award he won not so many years ago, after he gets off the phone with his estranged teenage daughter.

Day after day I worked with these remarkably talented, lost, incredible people—all brought together by food. It seemed that cooking was made for them, same as it was for me. They could work for a month or a year anonymously, get their shit together, and move on. Or not. It was a good lesson, because in the world I grew up in, you were expected to know what you were doing *now*. Not sometime after your twenty-ninth birthday. Hanging with these new work friends was a wake-up call. These were cooks, not chefs. What I did with my new skills was going to be up to me. It had never felt like that in the corporate world. I was unshackled, yet terrified by my newfound power of choice. A classic case of "be careful what you wish for."

While I was toiling in a basement with sixteen-gallon stainless-steel stockpots for a less than honest wage, my wife was thriving. Not only was she cutting the heads of the luminaries we used to gawk at on Spring Street, she was also providing our insurance and paying our bills, all the while buying me countless cookbooks and food magazines and circling new restaurant reviews for places we should try on my next day off. She was totally selfless even as I was barely contributing to our daily nut. What's more, cooking, I was gone fourteen hours a day and starting to feel guilty about it. Things are never what you imagine them to be, and I had not integrated that into the plan, as if there ever was a plan. Still, I was invested in the leap of faith that this was all headed somewhere.

Just when that old helpless feeling was becoming overwhelming, my cooking school instructor, Carrie, stepped in. She called out of the blue to tell me that I must connect with her husband, Ben. Though he had once flown helicopters in the Israeli Army, he was now the sous chef at an insanely busy uptown eatery called Yellowfingers—an Italian-style café that had just gone through a food makeover with a famous 1980s chef-consultant out of San Francisco. This chef had created the "farcita"—a sort of focaccia club sandwich that the north-of-57th-Street crowd had gone positively mad over.

Yellowfingers was primely situated on the corner of 60th Street and 3rd Avenue, across from the notorious Bloomingdale's department store. It had been designated *the* canteen for weary uptown shoppers. The ceiling-to-floor window walls opened wide to the street and the avenue. The afternoon I walked into the place for my meeting, I had to literally fight my way through a herd of full-length fur coats schlepping enormous fancy shopping bags with the letter "b" silk-screened on the side. Not exactly my crowd, but still it was easy to see this could be a real opportunity. What's more, Yellowfingers was part of a larger food conglomerate that included the upscale establishments Contrapunto, a bustling pasta joint; Arizona 206, the groundbreaking Southwestern eatery; and the grande dame of the empire, Sign of the Dove, where my family's old friend Andrew worked. It had not taken me long to come nearly face to face with the chef who had given me such practical career advice only a year earlier.

My meeting with Ben at Yellowfingers lasted maybe fifteen minutes. He was soft-spoken, mild-mannered, tall, and muscular. He gave the impression that during his military tour he had seen some shit you wouldn't want to. He possessed a calmness that transcended the mayhem of the bustling dining room. The guy was obviously knee deep. Two days later I found myself sandwiched between two swarthy Pakistani guys on the salad station, staring nervously out of the open kitchen where the line of well-heeled customers stretched a dozen deep out the door onto East 60th Street.

What had I done now? I have this awful habit of toiling diligently to get exactly what I want, getting it, and then spending all of my time trying to get out of it. How on earth would I get out of this one? There was no time to worry about it, though; I had salads to make.

Rezbi ran the cooking line. He was a decent enough guy for a sadistic prick armed with a big knife and a small amount of responsibility. I could just sense his glee when he saw me, the new guy. I was greeted with an unintelligible grunt even as I was left for dead.

I was assigned to work the "middle" station—aptly named because the workspace was jammed between an 800-degree pizza oven on one side, and, on the other, a thirty-six-inch charbroiler and six-burner stove with an oven underneath. I had two bubbling industrial fryers behind me and a lowboy fridge in front with mise en place for about ten menu items: diced tomatoes, chicken for various salads precooked in every conceivable way—roasted, grilled, and poached—sliced onions, olives, dressings, orange segments, salad mix, romaine lettuce, croutons, Arugula, grated Reggiano, the works.

The Caesar salad with calamari "croutons" was a bestseller at Yellowfingers, and Rezbi made it clear that I would get it right or else. Recipe and instructions were not included in that order. This was watch and learn—fast! You open the lowboy refrigerator drawer at your knees that is loaded with calamari that's been cleaned and cut into rings, now soaking in milk. Grab a fistful or two and throw it into a cornmeal, flour, and herb mixture. Shake off the excess in the fry basket, ignoring the cloud of flour emanating over your head. Drop the wire basket containing the sticky ringlets into a gas-fired fryolator tanked up with 350-degree pure canola oil. The steam blasting from the moist squid hitting the hot oil had a way of opening up all your pores, allowing for a very alternative sort of facial. Repeat forty-seven more times, all the while preparing the other nine items on your station.

Rezbi would scream, "Four field greens, three calamari, make that five calamari, six, now ten!"—and this went on without pause for hellish hours of midtown lunch or, if on the night shift, until midnight.

"Four more arugula. Let's *go*, Habibi." My hands were so caked in corn-meal that it took the dull side of a chef's knife to scrape it all off after the shift. Not to mention half a tube of Clinique Men's Scrub to remove the calamari steam from my face, purchased at Bloomingdale's, during a five-minute break, from an attractive young clerk in a black scoop-neck sweater whom I recognized from the restaurant the day before. She soon became a regular, providing me with a steady stream of free Clinique samples. I was starting to think that she wanted more from me than the occasional gratis calamari salad, but then again, I was mostly clueless about what women wanted from me in the first place.

Facial pores aside, the move uptown was proving to be a good one. I was now working double shifts, a practice so common they might as well have just called it one. You really grew to understand why cooks smoke and drink so much. Sometimes that stolen five-minute break is the only way you knew lunch had ended and dinner had begun.

New York's Upper East Side was wall-to-wall humanity in front of Bloomingdale's every evening around six p.m. when the Manhattan workforce collided with the throngs of hungry shoppers. It was absolute trial by fire in that kitchen, and Rezbi would just look at me with this de-monic smile and shrug. He had such a vendetta for me, but it was noth-ing like the one he had for some of these young cooking-school grads who just sauntered in. They'd show up with their clean-shaven faces and pressed chef whites and checked pants and shiny clogs—Leatherette knife bag with the school's insignia on the side, which translated, as far as Rezbi was concerned, to "know-nothing asshole." He would taunt the new guys mercilessly, and halfway through a shift you could see they weren't going to cut it. They would rather be at Daniel, or Bouley, or Jean-Georges. I would have, too, but I wanted to cook, now!

The youthful, cooking-school-attitude guys didn't last long in Rez-bi's domain. I'd be dousing my hands in cornmeal for the eight thou-sandth time of the day, and out of the corner of my eye I'd see him eviscerating one of them. An hour later I'd notice the poor kid secretly packing up his elaborate knife kit, asking where the bathroom was, and the next thing you knew, he'd be sneaking out the door in shame, humiliation, or just plain fear. This was no place to learn execution or finesse. It was cooking in the extreme—an open kitchen with the front door right there—and I swear sometimes these aspiring culinary upstarts would pull their coats up over their heads like gangsters caught in a sting, crawling out with their faces hidden.

Their humiliation was my motivation. There was no chance that that was going to be me. So six days a week I did everything I could to keep up, make good, and stay employed. No one is rooting for you at this level, except, of course, the sous chef, because he's the schmuck who will have to do your job if you bail—although our sous chef, Ben the ex-Israeli soldier, was far from a schmuck. One day while making a mother lode of pastry dough, a pastry assistant got her ponytail caught in the paddle of the fifty-quart Hobart mixer, twisting and ripping it out from the roots. This poor girl went into shock as the entire kitchen staff stood there motionless, blood everywhere. Ben, however, took charge, administered first aid, and comforted her until EMS arrived. He all but saved her life. I could barely look.

Under less dire circumstances, the cooks, the dishwashers, even the porters make sport of seeing who they could skewer and put out with the trash. The kitchen was worse than high school for cruel practical jokes. They'd turn up the temperature on the pizza oven when you weren't looking, scorching your handiwork, which you only noticed when smoke started to fill the dining room. Or worse, some shithead would turn the heat off under the stock you'd been slaving at for three hours, leaving you with a ruined vat of cold, congealed fat.

Twelve hours a day I was up to my ass in calamari, cornmeal dough, and anchovies, and it sucked and yet was exhilarating at the same time. So what if my take-home pay was less than ninety bucks a day. I was surviving and in the game. Even the fussy, uptown crowd didn't bother me after awhile. "This pizza is too crunchy. Too soggy. Too spicy. Split this in two plates. No dressing. Dressing on the side. No garlic, no oil, no butter. Extra this, none of that." I got one order from a woman who, according to the waiter, wanted her steak cooked half medium-well, and the other half rare. Sorry, lady, my magic wand is in the shop.

I'd been at it for several months when one day, while dicing chicken with my brand-new Japanese hybrid knife from Bridge Kitchen Supply around the corner, the knife slipped and I gashed my hand just below my thumb almost to the bone. Complete Asshole move, no doubt in part because I was paying a little too much attention to that Bloomingdale's girl who was seated in full view of the kitchen in that damn scoop neck. There was blood, a lot of blood, all over the station cutting board, and it would not stop. The line for a seat is spilling out the restaurant door, and no matter that I'm bleeding profusely, clearly I'm going to have to cook. Rezbi notices my finger and actually looks concerned, which tells me that it must be really bad.

He says in his Pakistani English, "Finger cut very bad, should to go home, but you are cook, so we do." Translation? They helped me wrap the wound and stanch the blood flow, slapped a rubber glove on my bad hand, and for the rest of the night I was right there getting caked with cornmeal flour, milk, and blood and all under wraps, same as always. It was a calamari salad campfire night, all warm and fuzzy. I knew I had crossed some boundary with the staff. They would have rather worked themselves half to death alone than acknowledge one ounce of respect to an outsider like me. Suddenly I was no longer considered a pussy. I was initiated with my own blood.

With this newfound nonpussyhood, the learning curve ramped up significantly. I'm from a proud immigrant family, and for me manning the pizza station was a natural fit and a blessing in disguise. With Ben at my side I learned to make dough the right way, just the perfect mix of warm water, flour and olive oil and yeast. Even Rezbi could see it was really good. I found myself making fifty pies a day. At last this felt like it had a direction to it.

I was actually starting to dig watching Rezbi cook, now that I didn't feel like he was out to get me all the time. A complete madman, he would have a dozen preparations going at once, with four or five sauté pans all boiling away. Pasta, chicken, several fish dishes, a mixed grill with sausage and lamb, all of them plated and ready to go in a flash. They weren't always picture perfect, but speed was the thing here. I watched him in awe while I sweated it out on the pizza line. All those days of coming in early and working hard were starting to pay off, both in my cooking skills and the small bit of respect in the trenches it earned for me.

I worked all the stations at Yellowfingers for several months. I was on nights from two to twelve, and Gina was working in SoHo from ten in the morning until eight or nine. After her long day, she'd schlep into the city from Brooklyn to pick me up in our aging Mazda. Times were tough and yet they were easier. We'd piss away our salaries at the Subway Bar or Blue Ribbon, or the new Union Square Café, where I was learning to really eat and really drink for the first time in my life. We'd order the five-course tasting menu and it would be a fortune for us, but we didn't care. Whatever the rules were back then, we weren't living by them and that felt fine.

The only thing really nagging at me was my age. You've got to be hungry to move ahead in this business and I knew I had started late. About ten years too late. If I didn't ask for what I wanted, I might end up picking cornmeal out from beneath my nails for a good long time. So I approached Ben, who had been so decent to me in the past, and asked if he might have anything new coming up. He didn't, but he told me to snoop around next door at one of the sister restaurants, Arizona 206. Andrew, from Sign of the Dove, had recently become the executive chef of the entire conglomerate. Up to this point I had been reluctant to ask him for help. With his less than encouraging words still ringing in my ears, I had a lot to prove to him, and myself, that I had the balls to stick with it. On the other hand, I didn't want any preferential treatment. Not that that was likely. Andrew had already demonstrated himself to be a straight-up kind of guy. What's more, regardless of whose son I was, it was doubtful nepotism would get you far in a professional kitchen. Too many sharp objects and the job. Screw up and you're going to be out on your ass. So I cranked up the courage and asked Andrew for a job, which turned out to be a valuable lesson. A crazed chef in a new gig will take any skilled help he can get. Andrew offered me the seven a.m. slot, which meant I'd be on the grill station for the lunchtime shift. Maybe not the best job in the city, but it was a break. I had scraped the last bit of cornmeal from beneath my nails, at least for a while.

# South by Southwest

My start at Arizona 206 was a lesson in diplomacy and humility. Having come from trial-by-Rezbi, I was feeling pretty full of myself. That was until I met Joan, the cook who was purportedly given the task of bringing me up to speed.

Hard as it may be to believe, New York in the early nineties had barely discovered the flavors of the Southwest. What offerings there were tended to be ethnic hole-in-the-wall places that, while sensationally authentic and sometimes delicious, fell more under the category of Tex-Mex than true, stylish Southwestern cooking. The city was just in the infancy of its foodie revolution back then, and there was room for real creativity and experimentation. Chefs like Mark Miller, who ran Coyote Café in Santa Fe and Red Sage in Washington, D.C., and Brendan Walsh, who put Arizona 206 on the map, were blazing the way, leaving a trail of chilies and chipotle and all kinds of interesting new ingredients in its wake. I began at 206 just after Brendan had bailed following a wildly successful run. A woman named Cheri had inherited the chef's mantle and was left with the remnants of what was once a very good kitchen staff. Several were women on the culinary fast track, and I'm sure Joan was one of them. She certainly was high enough up the food chain to have exactly zero interest in me.

Arizona 206, like Yellowfingers, drew its clientele from the Upper East Side's women of leisure, handsome financiers, their wives and mistresses, and the occasional aging rock star. All were desperately in search of New York's finest Southwestern food. It seems this demographic is always in search of something. This was good, because it gave young cooks like Joan palates on which to work their unique magic. I started at the grill station under her watch. Unfortunately she had better things to do than share any of her magic with a rank amateur like me.

The Arizona 206 kitchen was as small as a box. The stoves and stainless-steel cooking tables were set up facing one another in an island-like fashion. The place was so cramped there was nowhere to run and hide, and I found myself adrift without a clue what to do. I needed a mentor, fast. Working directly across from me was one of the few other male cooks in the place, Eric, a graduate of CIA long before it became the glamour-cooking academy it is today, churning out talent candidates for the Food Network farm team. He was a seasoned professional with a three-star New York City pedigree who had worked within the hallowed walls of Le Bernardin, Le Côte Basque, and many other revered establishments with a "Le" in the title. Needless to say, he knew something about food. Not that there was any chance I'd be privy to that. The first thing he said when he realized I wasn't an errant delivery boy was, "What the fuck are *you* doing here?" At least Joan did not greet me with Eric's acerbic tone. She merely acted that way.

I have no doubt women are conceptually swifter than men, hence their ability to multitask better. In the case of a busy kitchen, they can manage the numerous components of an elaborate dish better than most guys—and that included me at this neophyte stage. Once I got someone to actually recognize that I was employed here as a cook, I needed to learn the plating and the pickups—the actual setup of the food on the plates. Cheri's menu was complex and featured numerous components, each cooked separately. There were several "three-pan pickups," meaning three separate pans for every dish prepared: one for the protein, one for the accompanying vegetable, and one for the garnish. Multiply this by the number of dishes going out to the dining room at any one time and it's a tricky logistical cooking challenge. It was a long way from pizza and salad.

We were doing an adobo-marinated saddle of rabbit wrapped in caul-fat (fatty stomach membrane of pig) in cumin-spiced glaze with a corn chipotle relish on a bed of polenta. One of Joan's underlings, the woman working alongside me, not only had done this a thousand times before, but she was just faster than me all around. You could tell she knew the plating in her sleep—the polenta here, the relish there, the saddle sliced on the bias, and boom, you've got it. I was new to this level of finesse and needed instruction, diagrams, and practice desperately.

While Joan was steadfastly ignoring me, "Le" Eric was busy hurling blazing hot sauté pans over my head, en route to the pot sink behind me. This was risky business. If you got wrapped up in a chore for two seconds and lost track of him, a twelve-inch sauce pot would sail dangerously close overhead like an errant missile. He seemed unconcerned that the hot oil he'd used to sauté whatever was in the dripping pan, sprayed out on me in midflight. It would hit the bottom of the empty, thirty-six-inch-deep pot sink with a jarring crash. I looked up at him incredulously, but he was unfazed. He just kept on quietly cooking and heaving pots, in his own angry little world. My nerves were already on edge. The crashing, foundry-like reverberations of All-Clad on steel hardly helped.

Was this some kind of test, I wondered? No one else really seemed to notice. Maybe it was one more hazing ritual for the new kid. Joan finally started to pay some attention to me. She would come back into the kitchen every half hour or so, fault me for everything from my knife techniques to my abject failure at making sweet potato fries, and then mosey back to whatever it was she had been doing. All of a sudden I found myself missing my old job. I began to wonder how I was going to fit in here.

There are many colorful personality types that gravitate toward the job of cook. Eric ruled his domain by intimidation and fear. Monica, on the other hand, ruled by sheer sexuality. She was about the hottest thing in a chef coat and would wear her immaculate white one a size too small, just in case any of the prep guys didn't notice her ample bust line, tiny waist, and derrière as round as a pumpkin. The guys loved watching her at the stove, licking their chops as if she were a slice of cream pie, and to them in their mostly thankless jobs, I suppose she was. As a cook, she was unflappable. Her knives were razor sharp, her skills impeccable. All of her meats came out perfectly: rosy duck breasts, succulent quails, rare venison. She got the job done without fuss, and the staff responded to her with respect, even if they were more interested in figuring out how they might get to see her naked.

I was still trying to figure out who to turn to for guidance in the middle of this stage play we called a kitchen. One thing I knew, you couldn't let Cheri see that you were sinking. If you had any hope of moving up, you'd better not be a burden to the chef. Joan, per usual, was completely unavailable to me. Monica was fast and efficient and her station ran like a dream, but I'm pretty sure she hadn't noticed that I even existed. Eric, on the other hand, seemed to be having a field day terrifying me. Not exactly an inviting environment. Maybe I could just remain invisible and pick up Southwestern cooking by osmosis.

Barely a week into this mess and Andrew decided to show up and see how I was doing. The timing could not have been worse or better, depending on your perspective. Lunch service had just begun and I already had three rabbits, two chickens, and a blazing plancha going for some wild rice corn cakes, which had to be molded by hand and cooked to order. I'm one sautéed chicken breast short of a panic attack when Andrew materializes out of thin air and notices that I'm lagging far behind. He takes a look at my disaster of a station and he is pissed, not only because I'm screwing up, but because no one had stepped up to make sure the rookie was trained properly. This was bad management and bad news for the chef more than for anyone else. But I didn't want to be the snitch. Not on Cheri, not on Joan, not on anyone. I'd rather take the fall then get a rap as a spoiled rookie whiner.

Andrew could have given up on me right then, but he took pity, not out of any familial obligation but more to protect the reputation of the place he was now responsible for as executive chef. He saw the carnage I was making of a rabbit breast I was trying to brown and he stepped in to help. This was like the pope teaching a new priest how to hear confessions. I had known of Andrew practically my whole life and had heard how proud his parents were. Now I could see why.

The breast meat was losing definition on its hatch marks because the sweet marinade on the rabbit was soiling the grill. Andrew asked me for the grill brush, which of course I had moved an hour ago in my panic to get organized. I reached under the stove where I had stupidly put it and to my horror found nothing left but a few charred bristles and a puddle of bubbling, molten toxic plastic that was beginning to stink up the kitchen.

Andrew was not amused. And if I thought I was going to get preferential treatment because his dad and my dad had been best friends for fifty years, guess again.

*"You have to be fucking kidding?"* he said. Ignoring me completely, he grabbed a dish towel with a pair of tongs, stuck the towel in the boiling fryer and scooped up a dollop of bubbling fat. In one deft motion he scrubbed the grill with the fat-soaked towel, sending out a plume of

flame like the exhaust of a fighter jet. "OK?" he said, and just looked at me. I nodded.

He took the next thirty minutes and walked me through the mise en place and plated a half-dozen menu items. He talked me through each step, spelling it out in a fashion anyone could understand. He demonstrated the entire where, how, and why of the way this well-oiled operation had to run. He got all the food out in about five minutes—a job that had been taking me ten minutes a plate. And then he was gone without a trace. I stood there wiping the sweat off the back of my neck, disoriented, trying to figure out what had happened, and whether I still had a job.

In midtown Manhattan, people are busy and even the finest cuisine has to be delivered to the table fast and efficiently. If some Park Avenue assets manager misses his two o'clock conference call because I can't get his adobo rabbit to him on time, he's never coming back. This is a death sentence in a competitive dining market. Andrew conveyed this urgency and taught me in thirty concentrated minutes what no one else in this crazy place had had the time to impart over the course of a week.

It also became apparent that everything at Arizona 206 was not as it seemed. Sure, we had landed some favorable reviews and we had good buzz on the street, but behind closed doors the kitchen was in disarray. I thought my first professional, upscale experience would be an orchestrated ballet of culinary perfection. Instead I ended up with a slapstick comedy complete with hurled projectiles. No restaurant can thrive for long under that kind of chaos. That was reinforced by Ricky's presence in a kitchen where normally a partner and busy executive chef would rarely show his face before dinner. Clearly this was a listing ship. Joan already had one foot out the door. Cheri was being overseen by her boss, her confidence dwindling with each passing meal period. Eric was storming about in his own private, pot-flying hell like a homeless madman muttering on the subway. About the only person who seemed unscathed was Monica, but none of us was privileged enough to know what was going on beneath her pristine chef's smock. Mainly the place had a mildewy feel to it, like something was off. No surprise, by the end of my second week, word came down. Cheri was out. We had a new chef.

# Benediction

When word gets out that your chef, John DeLucie, is doing some of the best tuna tartare in town (all that creamy avocado and zingy heat!), plus a hefty and juicy pork chop, a classically blissful Dover sole, an addictive clam chowder, a gorgeous fillet of wild salmon (with those adorable little beluga lentils) and such feloniously fatty short ribs, won't there be even more lemmings tumbling down the steps from Bank Street and through the door?

—Frank Bruni, *The New York Times*

 Suffice it to say, Frank Bruni's ode to Graydon Carter and, by association, my role at The Waverly did not hurt. Not that it made any difference. We couldn't possibly have been busier.

In essence, we had two parallel shows going on every evening. In the back, we were becoming a well-oiled cooking machine. The kitchen staff seemed pleased that our work was well reviewed. I brought the article back and read the highlights aloud. Domingo, my daytime sous chef, translated in Spanish, sentence by sentence as the good news unfolded. The rest of the guys paused for a moment, glugging their Latin American Kool-Aid concoction that they kept stocked in gallon-size industrial stainless-steel soup tureens scattered about the kitchen. Who knows what they put in the stuff, but it was always present and kept everyone hydrated. My Spanish is passable, but I'm hardly fluent. Based on the reaction to Domingo's colorful translation, I'd say the guys were amused, if not outright pleased.

Out in the dining room, where the place was filling up as usual, guests who had already gained "regular" status were reading Bruni's praises off of their BlackBerrys and congratulating the waitstaff with hugs and kisses. I stepped out into a regular love fest. We popped champagne and all at once movie stars and writers and neighborhood schoolteachers and dentists and even Eddie—the West Village homeless guy we cooked for almost every night, who remained perched near the kitchen window—celebrated in unison.

Gratifying as it was, however, the break was short-lived. My guys were there by merit of their skilled hard labor, not because of any spotlight being shone on them, and in no time the kitchen was cranking up to breakneck speed again. It takes a while for a kitchen to find its professional legs, and these guys were pros. We all worked in lockstep, measuring our evenings by how well we survived. Did everything go out on time? Was it cooked perfectly? Did anything come back, and if so, what the hell did we do wrong and how could we not do it again? As a team, we barely knew who was out front enjoying themselves. We cooked, we plated, we hustled. We busted our asses in a kitchen no doubt half the size of the ones in our customers' apartments and vacation homes, and it was all in a day's work.

From my catbird seat, however, I was aware there was a whole other game shaping up. The media was positively tripping over itself about the alleged drove of stars who crossed our hallowed threshold. I was mostly impervious to it. When you've lived in New York all your life, you get used to seeing famous people. They jump in cabs and order their eggs over easy at local coffee shops and go to the Union Square farmers' market for flowers and artisanal cheese, organic veggies, and farm-fresh eggs just like the rest of us. It was one of the great things about the city. It took a lot to get you to notice anyone.

One insanely busy evening I was surveying the action in our comfortably cramped dining room from my perch, jammed between the kitchen pass and a wall rack of very pedigreed wines that were probably worth more than the purchase price of my apartment. I saw Emil, looking dapper as always, leading a large party into the main room. The ceilings of The Waverly are fairly low, and as always the level of chatter was high. But as this party walked in, a hush fell over the room. That caught my attention.

I instantly recognized the signature silver ponytail and aviator sunglasses of the artistic director of Chanel, Karl Lagerfeld. He was outfitted in a tight black suit and what appeared to be a puffy, white, ruffled pirate's shirt with an enormous collar and bolo tie. Despite the fact that it was a perfectly warm evening outside, he wore his trademark fingerless biker gloves covered with, from my view, silver studs and a large zipper on the palm side of each one. The Godfather of haute couture glided his one-hundred-ten-pound frame across the floor, elegantly followed by his apostles, and come to think of it, there might have actually been twelve of them coming for supper. This was some deep fashion shit. Half of me was blown away by the effect he had on this room of mega-celebrities unto their own right—I had never seen so many halted conversations—and the other half was thinking I better get back to the kitchen and make some food. Still, I could not avert my gaze.

Mr. Lagerfeld and his alternate-universe entourage took their seats at the largest table we could crib together in the small space. Their very competent waiter was an actor-in-training named Michael, and I could tell from across the room that he was fighting the flop sweats, even as he prepared for the biggest audition of his serving career.

"The chef has prepared some additions to the menu this evening.

Would you like to hear them?" I could read his lips going over the requisite presentation. The King nodded attentively. "For an appetizer, we have a wild mushroom Arborio rice cake with a sunnyside quail egg and shaved parmigiano Reggiano. Next, for an entrée, we have a fillet of day-boat cod with a ragout of local fingerling potatoes, chanterelle mushrooms, and leeks braised in a little butter and white wine. Finally, for dessert, the chef has prepared poached apricots in mulled Pinot Noir with vanilla gelato." Michael paused to catch his breath. So far, so good. "There are several other new options available on the menu this evening," he continued. Karl Lagerfeld listened raptly, his studded gloved hands crossed in gentle repose. The rest of his table sat in silence as if waiting for his eminence to speak. When Michael finally finished his recitation, I could almost feel his sigh of relief. He closed by asking what every waiter is trained to ask before taking the order.

"Are there any questions?"

Michael looked around this enormous table of hungry faces, who in turn were looking to their fabled host. When Lagerfeld spoke, it was silent enough in the clubby dining room for every last soul to hear his words. "We have no questions at this table," he announced. "Only answers."

The Waverly buzz returned to its normal decibel. Michael survived his brush with high design and went to the computer to start typing in the very lengthy order, of which he had taken copious notes to get it right. I raced back to the kitchen and got Angel and the bandanna-clad, sweating crew working to get's KL's order done, fast. It might have been a little awe-inspiring to be serving one of the more influential Tables of Twelve dining in the city that night, but we still had a restaurant full of customers who also demanded and deserved exactly the same treatment. This is when you find out what your staff is all about. To an outsider, our cramped kitchen might have looked like pandemonium. But while next year's fashions were being decided in our dining room, in the back we cooked, plated, and served what would be an excellent meal.

Following the Last Supper, the next day we received a call from Karl Lagerfeld's office—a special order for takeout carrots, nothing more— just our roasted carrots to go, every day for a week. The black town car arrived promptly at noon.

# Twelve Smoking Ducks

Places turn over so fast in New York that you need to have your radar finely tuned, because when the shit hits the fan, the best cooks are already gone and on to the next big thing. My first foray into fine dining could have turned into a career disaster that left me abandoned in the charred wreckage. But under the new leadership of David Walzog, all of a sudden things began to change.

David came to Arizona 206 from Mark Miller's Red Sage in Washington, D.C., where he had been turning heads for several years. He was a wunderkind and, reportedly, a "super cocky young fuck" (as one of our remaining sous chefs remarked). I think half the kitchen was out to get him before he unpacked so much as a paring knife. However, once he got his feet on the ground, things began to change drastically.

My immersion into Southwestern food was an eye-opener. I thought I knew a thing or two about the roots of good homegrown cooking by merit of my Italian heritage. Take garlic, for example. To an Italian it means fat pale cloves sliced razor thin and simmering in extra-virgin olive oil, filling the house with the aroma of the gods. One whiff could bring me back decades to my grandmother's kitchen, a five-year-old squirt tugging on her apron begging for a taste of whatever it was that was simmering, sizzling, crackling, or bubbling over my head on the stove. It was a rare day when I was growing up that the scent of garlic was not permeating the home, while we waited for Grandpa to get home from one of the three fruit and vegetable markets he owned in downtown Brooklyn. But here at 206, the basics took on a whole new meaning for me—a piquancy and vibrancy tempered with lime and inflamed with chilies and cumin and turmeric. Walzog was dripping with this sensibility, plus he was young and aggressive, and I identified with him. He wanted to rock the boat and turn the place on its ass. As well as new ingredients, he brought new structure, discipline, people, and huitlacoche (corn fungus), which he cleverly incorporated into a delicious sausage and which I eagerly signed on to make every other day.

Making sausage is everything I like about cooking. You take raw ingredients, cut them up with your bare hands, and mold them into a mishmash where the product doesn't look like anything you'd choose to eat. From that, you end up with something remarkable and delicious. It is a lost art. Even today, I often walk over to Salumeria Biellese on 8th Avenue, where third-generation Italians still make sausage the old way. It's nostalgic for me to see the gnarled, deeply lined faces of the guys who remind me of my grandfather. They are perfectionists—artisans who do it the only way they know—the right way, by hand.

At 206 our prep kitchen was manned by an entirely new generation of Mexican cooks who were doing most of the heavy lifting. What a great and colorful lot they were to hang out with. I'd hunker down with my hombres, cutting fatback into squares, along with garlic, pork butt, and herbs, all stuffed into the chute of the grinder that would churn out the sausage. You'd put the stuffer mechanism on the end of the machine—basically a long, hollow, round tube—and then take the sausage casing and just like the directions on a condom wrapper, roll it all the way down to the base and let her rip. This was when I first started to feel like I was becoming an integral part of a team. Sausage making was good, honest, satisfying work.

After a morning of this, I'd return to the main kitchen to gear up for lunch. Working for David was a whole new experience. For such a young guy (younger than I was, anyway), he had an attitude years beyond his age. No preening or shouting or biting anyone's head off. He'd call out, "Johnny, cook me up a duck breast. Here, slice it this way, halfway through, and twist it up like that and let's see what it looks like." He had this mellow, practical attitude, and his preparations looked and tasted great. He led by example, getting everyone in the kitchen involved in the menu. He knew enough to leave the dishes that were working in place while tweaking the weaker ones, and he was bringing a whole new energy to the menu. We were doing things with guinea hen and poblano chilies and tomatillos, and the food was taking on real character.

So was the atmosphere in the kitchen. Like any organized hierarchy, there was some dissent and bad feelings from the staff. People aligned with Cheri were upset, and people who had been there awhile were in fear of their jobs and wanted no part of change. Me, I have always managed to embrace the new, the different, and the odd. David and I were cool, if for no other reason than because I was the only newcomer he had. I was working hard, taking direction, and had no attachment to the old ways. One afternoon he said to me, "Dude, gotta work nights. That's where the action is," and next thing I knew, I was done with my 5:30 a.m. wake-up calls.

Over the next few months I gained a chef's primer in teamwork, and to this day I owe David for his very engaged style of kitchen management. Don't get me wrong, he could rip you a new one just like any other chef. He would lose his patience with me, but more often than not I deserved it. I remained incredibly dense about the new pickups, and I just couldn't remember what went with what. Was it the chicken with the hominy or did it go with the quail? Too busy and too embarrassed to ask yet again, I put the plated food up with the accompaniment ass-backwards. He went berserk on me. I would have gone berserk on me. Eventually I got it right.

I remember one particular night near closing. We had been there since noon, and fatigue was beginning to wreak havoc on motivation. This was the time when most of the staff is cleaning up, dressing down, or one step removed from hitting their stash. We were basically out the door when the kitchen printer starts to rattle with a new order. David shouts, "Listen up!" The hostess bobs her head into the little window between the kitchen and dining room and asks if any of us spoke Japanese. Trouble approaching. Apparently, twelve Japanese tourists had descended on us, guidebooks in tow, and since everything we do in the end is about maximizing profit, it's not like the maître d' was going to turn away a group that size—even if they did slip in just under the wire.

It's the last table of the night, and we mobilize. We put our Coronas out of the way and start on the appetizers. Now it's a race: black bean terrines, barbecue pork tamales, tequila-cured salmon—all being made and plated at record speed. In order to save time, the waiter had rung in the apps first so we could get a head start. Now he raced back to the table to get the entrée order. Twelve ducks? This *must* be a mistake. Why would twelve people travel halfway around the globe, read about a celebrated American Southwestern restaurant in a Japanese/English food guide, and all order the same thing? Apparently the communication between the waiter and the party had broken down so badly that at the sound of the word "duck" there was consensus and excitement, and twelve people started to repeat the word "duck, duck, duck," nodding their heads enthusiastically in tandem. The waiter assumed, probably not so accurately, that duck is what they all wanted.

So David, who was as thrilled as I was about this late-night order, takes charge. He gets out this enormous rondeau, which is a pan that covers two full burners and can handle all twelve duck breasts at once.

We get them fired up in no time and the skins begin to render beautifully and the rondeau goes into the oven to finish. No sweat. We continue our station cleanup, and David kicks back with a glass of wine and starts telling the staff Red Sage war stories. Our cocktail party is just getting cozy when the closing waiter interrupts everything, running in from the dining room, flailing his arms, shouting, "Where's the main course?"

Fuck!

We had, of course, totally forgotten about it. We whipped open the oven and out came twelve smoking ducks. We ripped them off the sizzling rondeau with our bare hands in the desperate hope of slowing down the cooking process. For a second we wondered if we should cook twelve new ducks? It's midnight. Do we explain to our guests that their ducks had been overcooked because the staff had been dicking around instead of getting the food out? How do you say "dicking around" in Japanese, anyway? We teamed up to plate and oversauce and finesse the veggies so that twelve plates of toasted duck went out looking like the pictures in the Japanese New York City guidebooks. We held our breath, praying that these nice folks would not mind a little well-done duck for dinner. Thankfully, they dug in without complaint.

We all cracked into our second round of shift beers, and David thanked and praised every last member of the team for another great night on the job. He had been angry about the duck at first, but he knew that he was at least partly responsible. Not many chefs owned up that way.

I waltzed through my cleanup, wrapping the remains from the mise en place, changing all the containers and getting them ready for the morning shift. I carried all the perishables into the walk-in box in the basement and then returned to my station. I wiped down the stove and cleaned the gunk and particles out of the gaskets on all the refrigerator doors. We were responsible for cleaning everything above the floor, and it was tedious, shitty, important work that everyone hated, but you never knew when the city food inspector might show up. Sometimes we would bribe the night porters to do the cleanup in return for a little leftover ground pork with chilies. It was one of those unwritten rules that any chef would turn his head on if the amounts were negligible. I had a good rapport with the porters, whose rotten job it was to clean up after us, and I always valued the work ethic of the crew.

With the last surface wiped down and the icy shift beers firmly in hand, another busy night had come to an end. There was the usual banter among the staff about who was the most badass cook ever to stuff some braised rabbit into a tortilla. David waltzed off into the night seemingly pleased that this past-its-prime restaurant was once again growing in popularity, thanks to him.

I was about to book when Manny, a waiter who does standup comedy every Wednesday night at a little theater on the Upper West Side—the kind where the "talent" also works the lights and the curtain—pops his head in the kitchen. Before I can come up with a good excuse not to sit through another one of his late night "did ya ever notice this, did ya ever notice that" routines, he suggests something that actually sounds fun. One of our regulars—a well-heeled customer with boatloads of disposable income and too much time on his hands, invited some people down to his loft in Tribeca. Did we want to join? I was certainly too wired to go home.

I called Gina to ask if she wanted to come. No answer. She had been growing weary of hauling uptown, anyway, waiting for me to finish work. More often than not she had been on her feet all day and was understandably tired. I'd be all pumped on adrenaline, which was not a good mix with her exhaustion, so those dates had become a lot less frequent.

Our crew met up at a local watering hole to continue lubricating before the trip downtown. First thing in the door, I noticed Carla. She was the hostess at Yellowfingers, and I had forgotten about her since changing restaurants. She was a petite Latin beauty with a complexion the color of café au lait. She had big almond eyes, a bright white smile, and a very accessible vibe. I recall her being extremely friendly to guests and professional in her demeanor. She had once remarked to me that my eyes were the only ones she'd ever seen that were bigger than hers. I smiled politely and made ten more salads. I was a newly married man, and the less time spent around a pretty young girl like this, the better. Start buying into compliments like that, and you'll spend the next several months trying to pull your head out of your own ass.

I avoided eye contact, but Carla spotted me and waved me over to where she was nursing a weak-looking Cosmo, telling Manny the Comedian that she was having just one and going home. She pulls her stool right up close to me. I'm not much of a drinker, but something about Carla's eyes and her attention . . . and next thing I know I'm on my second gin and tonic and she is riveted by the story of how I dumped my nine-to-five to become a cook. I begin to get nervous and exhilarated at the same time by all of this unsolicited attention. When everyone announces they are ready to go, I give Carla a peck good night and feel like I'm off the hook. I'd brought the car in that morning and found a great space, so I offered to drive the troop downtown.

I leave the bar to retrieve the Mazda, drive around the block, and, to my horror and delight, find that Carla has decided to join the festivities and tag along. She opens the car door and pokes her head in—pretty hair flailing in all directions, hitting me in the cheek. The aroma of delicious tropical flora fills the tiny cockpit.

"You don't mind if I come along, do you," she states rather than asks, as she situates herself in the bucket seat next to me. Her skirt is short, legs shapely, and she is wearing painted-on textured tights, the kind that seem to be in fashion again and give away every muscular nuance of her thighs and calves. Manny and one of the other waiters sit in the back. I haven't done a thing wrong, and already I'm beginning to freak because Gina is going to smell this unfamiliar perfume and it's going to give me away. She'll ask about it, she'll probably know exactly what kind it is, and I'll be on the defense stand having committed the crime of giving my new friends a lift to a party.

We're nearly at the address and Manny wants to stop at the Korean market on Spring Street and buy beer. I pull over and the other waiter in the backseat decides he doesn't want to go to some "rich dickhead's" apartment after all. There is a great bar he remembers around the corner, and he gets out and disappears.

Now Carla and I are alone in the car making awkward small talk and my two drinks are definitely kicking in. This should feel all wrong but it doesn't. In fact, it feels all right, good in fact, which somewhere in the back of my head I know is wrong. Manny comes back with a cracked tallboy beer out of a six-pack and begins to bark directions. We pull up in front of a very expensive-looking renovation of a majestic old factory building that at some point in New York's history surely housed a business where things actually got made—clothing or sugar or the roasting of coffee beans. Ghosts of immigrants probably hide behind the Warhols and Hockneys that now line the walls. There's nowhere to park and Manny is out the door in a jiffy. Carla offers to ride around with me and look for a space, but I shoo her out the door, too. She is on the street leaning in, her long hair framing her face like an auburn picture frame. "See you up there?" she says cheerfully.

"Yeah, see you up there," I say in what I think is the most casual and noncommittal tone.

Manny and Carla disappear into the building. I take a deep breath and aim the Mazda straight for the Brooklyn Bridge.

# Blue Chili

I woke up at 10:30 the next morning with the kind of hangover that had nothing to do with alcohol. Gina was long gone. I should have been up showering, heading for the F train, getting on with my day. But I lay there instead thinking about why I had hightailed it back to Brooklyn with such urgency.

I had always been restless as a kid. Restless at everything. School. Studying music. Career. I was a master at moving on and I was no different romantically. Throughout high school, Gina had been the object of my desire. I craved her in a deep and carnal way, and the fact that she played hard to get and would have nothing to do with me made me want her more. When she decided to move to London to attend a top styling school, I dated around and ultimately got into a serious relationship with a lovely and responsible Fashion Institute of Technology graduate named Randi—a nice Jewish girl—the kind Mom wants you to marry, if Mom is Jewish, which culturally is a lot like Italian. My mom was thrilled. This made me even more restless than usual.

One of the many things I loved about Gina was that she was so headstrong and confident that there was no room for failure anywhere in her game plan. She got off that plane and decided our time was NOW.

I'd only been pining for her since high school, so it wasn't exactly like I put up a fight. Randi and I came to our rapid demise, and next thing I knew, Gina and I were a couple. Our path to marriage was no different. One second I'm planning a life of shul and dairy on Saturdays, next I'm planning a rehearsal dinner with rigatoni, ravioli, and linguini alla vongole on the menu. Sure, it crossed my mind that I should pause and reflect on this situation. I was not unhappy, far from it. Still, I wasn't sure I wanted to be married yet, and it crossed my mind that I could save everyone a lot of heartache by making the right decision here. The only problem was that the right decision felt an awful lot like the wrong decision. So I went with the only decision, which sure as hell seemed like the right one at the time.

I fought to put all these thoughts to rest on the train into the city and settled in for another invigorating day of roasting chilies and grinding sausage. I'd been at it for some time now, and while the learning curve had been good, I was getting this uneasy sense that I was not getting anywhere as far as some of the larger life issues were concerned. My chronic anxiety was making a return appearance, giving me fits of claustrophobia in the subway on my commute to work. I would take a few deep breaths outside the restaurant on arrival and get on with my day. Making a decent living was a concern. At BFC, I did well financially when I had my game on. The cable bill was paid and there was always a little something left over for an afternoon of shopping at Tower Records. My take-home pay at Arizona 206 was the same as it had been since I started, even though I had improved steadily and my skill set as a cook was expanding. So I decided to take things into my own hands.

That morning after I completed sausage duty, I wiped my greasy entrails-coated hands on my towel, hung it from my apron, and went looking for David. I found him walking quickly through the dining room with our bright-eyed hostess, decked out in so much funky jewelry that she went *clank clank clank* with every step. "Hey, Chef, gotta sec?" I asked.

"Nope. Wha' dya need?"

"I'm been thinking, ummm, since I've been working here a while for the same money and I—"

"Nope. Sorry, Johnny. Can't help ya." He went on his merry way.

My year-end review over, I returned to the kitchen with a scowl. I knew it wasn't personal. David liked me fine, but the last thing any chef wants is some cook busting his ass about a ten-dollar-a-day raise. I spent the rest of the afternoon gutting small birds, roasting peppers, grinding fresh chilies—the usual stuff you occupy your time with if you make Southwestern food. Evening fell, the place filled up, and I spent the next four hours working the grill. Rabbits on, rabbits off. Ducks on, ducks off. Chickens on, chickens off. I recognized my old gonna-fuck-this-up feeling washing over me, but I also sensed that my ultimate future was not in the Southwest. I needed someone to talk to and that someone was Eric, of all people—the pot-throwing madman. If anyone knew about going to the dark side, it was Eric.

When I had moved to the night shift, he suddenly became aware of my cooking skills and we had inexplicably become friends. I suppose like everyone else in this business, you just had to earn your chops. Someone else would step in as a target for his All-Clad projectiles.

After a few nights out, we discovered that we shared a love for music. Eric was a frustrated bluesman in a chef's toque, grinding it out in the kitchen by day, and hitting every club with a pickup blues band in the city by night. He was a completely misunderstood guy with his searing steel-blue eyes and a cold, stoic demeanor. He had everyone fooled because deep down he was a tortured, sensitive soul. He might appear to be one angry motherfucker if you didn't know him, but like so many in the trenches he apparently had a lot to be angry about. Cooks, in general, were not a cheerful, lighthearted bunch. Once I was out of range of Eric's projectile pots, we became tight, mainly because deep down I understood his ethic. Cook by day and play guitar by night. If only I were so focused.

I found Eric after my shift and settled in for the evening at his pre-war Upper West Side one bedroom. He took one look at my face, put a record on the turntable, picked up his guitar, and began to wail. We must have listened to a solid hour of Stevie Ray Vaughn, which Eric was partial to, while he played along and I marveled at the dexterity of his fingers on the maple neck of his Telecaster. In between tracks I cut loose about the lousy pay and the work and the terrible injustice of it all and how unappreciated I felt. Eric just sat there riffing away. He'd heard this all a thousand times before.

The thing is, Eric did not have bigger ambitions in the kitchen. He was burned out on the whole thing and remained detached, and for him that worked. Arguably, I could have used a little of that detachment therapy myself. But I wanted more.

Luckily, his girlfriend, Nancy, another member of the dysfunctional cooking tribe, happened to walk in at that moment. She was a lovely, earthy blonde with a penchant for baking and a skill for tolerating and appreciating Eric. She had just landed a pastry chef gig at a stylish new restaurant in the East 20s. Peter Legard, a French chef, was taking the helm. I hadn't heard of him but it didn't matter. I was ready to dive into something new. Nancy said she'd put in a good word for me.

What a strange and wacko fraternity this is, I thought while saying good night. Eight months ago I was introduced to this blues-riffing, pot-flinging madman who did everything in his power to intimidate me back into an office job. And here he was now, a sympathetic ear. A year later I stood up as best man at their wedding. It was all so fleeting, these affairs of the heart and stomach conducted in the late hours after a long night in a hot, steamy kitchen.

I hauled my tired ass to the subway, guitar licks still ringing in my head. All I could think about was my potential exit from the Arizona 206 family, and the people like Andrew, David, Rezbi, and Ben who had been so hard on me, for all the right reasons. I knew you had to be mobile to get ahead in this business, yet on the other hand I felt a real allegiance to these people. I got to the stoop of our brownstone and saw that all the lights were out in our apartment. It was one in the morning. I hadn't talked to Gina all day. I wondered whether she was even home.

# Gold Leaf and Turbot

As it turned out, Peter Legard had the big-time résumé: Petrossian, River Café, Le Louis XV in France, where he had trained under the eye of the legendary Alain Ducasse. I probably should have been nervous about my interview, but between my completely naïve and cocky attitude and Nancy's good word, I figured I was a shoo-in.

I showed up at Margaux to find a team of workers spackling, painting, hanging Sheetrock, and positioning the heavy oak bar. Nail guns were detonating like gunfire. I asked for the chef and a handyman with joint compound adhering to his shoes pointed toward the basement. I found Peter sitting in his makeshift office—two sawhorses with a door on top, scattered with requisition orders and résumés. He was barking food orders into the receiver of a brand-new, very modern phone system, the kind more geared toward elegant office showrooms than a restaurant basement. I sat down on an upright wine crate for the interview. Amid the flurry of nonstop calls he asked four basic questions: What's your training? What's on your menu? How do you cook it? What's your schedule? He actually seemed mildly impressed when I told him how business had surged at 206 and how busy we were, though

I had a feeling he was more interested in the competition from a fellow chef than anything else. Still, I guess he figured I couldn't be too terrible, because in between calls he offered me the position of poissonnier, and threw in a ten-dollar-a-day raise over my Arizona 206 salary to boot. He went back to his paperwork and I went home to Brooklyn to look up the word "poissonnier."

Margaux was the brainchild and passion of two brothers from Brooklyn who, rumor had it, made their fortune building and installing Corian countertops in oversize homes on suburban Long Island. They had clearly done something right, because they had rented an awfully big space for newcomers to the restaurant business, and they had engaged a top-drawer chef in Peter Legard. The cavernous floor plan required all of their elegant, high-end construction chops. These guys may not have had any experience in the food business, but at least they knew how to build. And they trusted Peter to pull together an A-list kitchen team and design a menu that would make the place a success.

I reported for my first day on the job apprehensive about my newfound calling for French food and wondering how in the world I was going to bluff my way through this jam. Instead, I was handed a tool belt and a pair of safety glasses and put to work power-sanding and spray-painting antique table bases with flat black Krylon paint. And I was not alone. Three new cooks and it seemed like a good-sized bus staff were all on their hands and knees as well. I guess with the ballooning budget, the two brothers had to trim the fat somewhere. It actually was gratifying in a way. We were forced to develop a sense of camaraderie and ownership almost immediately, which is the very least you could hope for with a start-up staff.

While we waited for the third finish coat to dry on the dining room floor, we kept an eye out for the Italian furniture that was due through U.S. customs. Meanwhile, the kitchen was being primed and finished. It was a spacious, heavy-duty affair lined with industrial Wolf French Top stoves. These were new to me. The double-wide, flat, cast-iron surface heats incredibly hot above small center circles, where the gas jets are. It becomes less intense as you move a pot or pan away from the center heat source. If you want to fire something red hot, you used the middle. The rest of the surface radiates heat, giving you a wide range of intensity. This was going to take some practice to get it right.

While the place came together, Peter was working himself into a frenzy designing the menu. Of course, my usual fears were nipping at my heels. The job of poissonnier is to be responsible for every fish dish on the menu. That was quite a daunting task, considering the level of food service we were about embark upon. Why he had assigned me— this not so young, neophyte to a French kitchen—as poissonnier? I could barely pronounce Maurice Chevalier.

One reason, I suppose, was because there are far fewer experienced cooks trained up to this level than you'd think. Also, there may have been a slight language barrier issue during my interview. I said that I had worked with duck and rabbit on the grill at 206. Duck and rabbit are delicate meats that require subtle handling. It's quite possible that Peter, with his so-so English, translated my delicate grill cooking experience into a compromise solution for his fish needs. And what I didn't know, he could beat into me with the assistance of two sous chefs.

As the menu took shape, Peter was doing some intense stuff in the kitchen and we had our hands full keeping up. We'd take ten cases of beefsteak tomatoes, which when piled up reached the ceiling, and we'd peel and seed and dice them up and reduce them down s-l-o-w-l-y with garlic and shallots and herbs to less than one gallon of sauce. This "fondue"—so called for its rich viscosity—was denser than the sun, and one teaspoon could change an entire sauce's landscape. Peter was, like I imagined every chef out of the Ducasse house, an insane perfectionist. You had to be with this food, it was all so expensive and complex. His recipes were like a house of cards. If one element was a little off, the whole dish collapsed.

He kept us hopping on tasks that to an outsider (for example, me) seemed almost beside the point. We'd brunoise garlic, taking every single solitary clove and dicing it seven cuts on the bias and five on the slant. This gave you perfectly squared one-eighth-inch by one-eighth-inch squares that ended up spooned into sauces with reckless abandon. It took forever to create them, and when you were on your twenty-fifth clove Peter would walk over, peer into the little stainless-steel pan where you stored your handiwork, and without a word dump the whole thing into a nearby garbage pail. "DO IT AGAIN!" he'd scream as he walked away. Once you survived the garlic siege, you'd find yourself delicately and painstakingly cleaning black trompette mushrooms and chanterelles with a tiny pastry brush and trimming freshly foraged cèpes. It was the same for every last vegetable.

Meanwhile the kitchen was filled day and night with friends of Peter and the two brothers, sampling these intricate, delectable concoctions, which Peter would then refine even more. One more thread of saffron to this, a drop more aromatic Banyuls vinegar to that. We were tweaking soups, pan juice broths, oxtail, seared cod cheeks—you name it.

I was assigned the task of making the nage—a very delicate bouillon teeming with fresh herbs and vegetables—for a striped-bass dish, from a scribbled handwritten recipe. This required taking a full case of white wine along with beefsteak tomatoes, onion, celery, leeks, parsley, thyme, chervil, and basil and simmering it so slowly that if there was a notion of a boiling bubble—if someone within five feet even *said* the word "boil"—the entire preparation would be ruined. Of course, every time I attempted this, all the asshole practical joker cooks would turn up the gas while I wasn't looking and get the thing rolling like a pot of spaghetti. I had to stand guard and fall behind on the seventeen other things I was supposed to be doing just to make sure we wouldn't have to pitch the entire broth. It finally got so bad that I was dismissed from my nage-making duties by Thomas, the sous chef, until he grew so tired of doing it that he reinstated me. We all were learning the ropes at Margaux. The chef was a talented narcissist and culinary psycho, but we were on board with his vision. The excitement of this food being brought to life was palpable.

Finally, the dining room was coming together in a big, if somewhat cheesy sort of way. High ceilings met columns bedecked in gold leaf, and the banquettes were stitched in a soothing shade of sea blue. The expansive bar was being finished to a shine that the folks at Johnson Wax would deem worthy. The owner/builders had a vision and apparently a budget large enough to leave no detail unattended to. PR people were securing VIP guests for the opening-night reservations, and the whole joint had the feel of a huge Broadway premiere.

There was major tension in the air as the big night drew near. Peter continued fiddling with the menu and we were making meal after meal that did not meet his standards of excellence and ended up in the trash, if not thrown against the wall in anger first. The French-tops often had thirty pots going on them at once. Cooks were fighting for equipment— food mills and cutting boards and graters. The scene was this hellish ballet of braising and boiling and blanching and grilling and sautéing. There were burns and cut fingers, panic attacks and exhaustion. Under-cutting the entire orchestration was the one overriding fear—the fear that every new restaurant owner and chef experiences to some degree. What if no one came? It is said that in New York City you can eat in a different restaurant every night for forty-six years without ever having to eat at the same place twice. It's no wonder new restaurant owners can be a little jittery.

Margaux debuted with a private, unofficial opening soiree for a warm and receptive crowd of friends and family, as well as a carefully

PR-orchestrated bunch of "walk-ins" from the street. The place looked and felt like a three-star restaurant and the food was miraculous. Gina came with a bunch of groovy gay fashion types in tank tops and skin-tight jeans doing their best to stand out and look cool in a very opulent but decidedly uncool place. I liked that about Gina and her friends. You couldn't miss them if you tried. The maître d' sat them in the back, so as to not offend anyone. Apparently the blue banquettes didn't quite match the tattoo ink on the arm of one of her guests. The place was packed, everyone raved about the food, and we deemed the night a huge success. Then we opened to the public.

We waited. And waited some more. We waited for the phones to ring. We waited for the walk-ins to come. We waited for the buzzy little snippets in the New York press that normally got people talking and showing up. We waited in vain. The buzz never came. Neither did the people. We had 120 seats to fill for lunch *and* dinner, a staff of two sous chefs on full salary, six hot cooks paid by the day, five cold cooks, a half dozen busboys, eight waiters, a manager, and a sommelier—and we were only doing thirty dinners a night. Even the guys folding the napkins could see that the payroll had to be eclipsing sales by a scary margin.

Peter was sweating bullets, but nothing like the Two Brothers, who had laid out the dough. And as if it wasn't horrible enough in the front of the house, the tension for all of us in the kitchen was over the top. We had nothing to do most of the time but look busy, avoid eye contact at all costs, and please our increasingly on-edge chef. The place was so empty at times, tumbleweed could have blown through. Cash was pouring out of the owners' pockets like water from an open spigot. Every day there were closed-door meetings and rumblings of menu change. Bad feelings abounded, and there was backstabbing and faultfinding and blame establishing. Surprisingly, the voice of calm turned out to be the chef, who stayed the course and convinced everyone to hang in there. One good review would change Margaux's fate, and Peter never doubted his food for a minute. So it was down to this. Apparently, our cherub-faced sommelier played in a zydeco band that featured *New York Times* food reviewer Bryan Miller. With a little persuasion, he was going to make sure his bandmate, Miller, found his way to Margaux to write a review. Soon.

# The Waverly Juice

In those first months at The Waverly, no one could get near the place. We were jammed to the rafters. The media collectively lampooned us for closing our doors to the public and running an exclusive club. Who knew the place was going to catch on fire with the most elite clientele to grace the pages of every major tabloid on the planet?

One evening around seven p.m., I decided to take my pre-dinner-crush stroll through the dining room. This is always the moment of calm before the storm—my chance to see how full we are, check out the reservation book, and figure out how many espressos I should drink. I might notice out of the corner of my eye if someone recognizable happens to be settling in for a nice potpie or a plate of Dover sole with vegetable sauté and hollandaise. But for me and the rest of the staff, it was all about meals and seatings and how to get the dinners out hot and keep the tables moving and everyone happy. No one would dare approach an über-famous celebrity, least of all me. For one thing, what would I say to them? "Nice hundred-million-dollar deal I read about in the *Journal* today. Bon appetit."

* * *

What's more, people in that unique orbit come to The Waverly for their own version of privacy. Unless someone has a specific question about the food, I don't pry. Managers, hostesses, and career waiters have been fired for being overly familiar with the guests. One very handsome and seemingly savvy host we employed thought nothing about sitting down at the table for an invited, after-dinner cocktail with the actor Will Smith. Emil had just entered the dining room with his hands clasped in trademark style behind his back, eyes peering over the top of his expensive frames. He walked over to the table in question, excused the interruption, and the following day excused the manager from his duties. No matter how you cut it, we are merely here to serve. You don't cross the line from friendly to familiar.

Espressos pumping, I finished my walkabout and was about to head back to my post in the kitchen, when a voice calls my name. "Johnny, how ya doin'?"

I recognize a regular whom I've met several times named Jimmy. None of us are quite sure what he does for a living, but he comes in often, and often with very famous and familiar faces. I didn't even know he knew my first name. Usually it was just "Chef." Now I'm trapped, so I walk over to say hey and see how his dinner was. No big deal. I'll do that several times a night with any regular customer, part of my job.

I shake hands with Jimmy and inquire about his cedar-plank trout. I smile at his guest, and then consciously try not to freeze up. I am one on one with a face that I can safely say would be recognized by every single person on the planet. There are only two or three famous people I would consider personally iconic, and whose work has moved me or changed my life in a particular way. This guy was at the top of the list.

"Have you met Bob?" Jimmy asks congenially enough. I chuckle out loud. No, I have not met Bob. I extend my arm out to shake his hand.

"Hello, Bob. How are you?" I say. He sticks his hand out cordially.

"How ya doin' kid? Great job!"

I walk back to the kitchen so jangled I can't even remember what I came out for in the first place. Have I met Bob? Of course I haven't met Bob. Where would I have met Bob? *Ya talking to me? You talking to me? There's no one else in the room. Ya must be talking to me.* Even in Puebla, Mexico, where many of our hardworking line cooks hail from, they all know *El Taxi Driver*.

The personalities we drew weren't just well known. They were the names and faces so far up the entertainment, literary, and fashion food chains that even *celebrities* couldn't get callbacks from these people. They were the movie stars who drove the box office. The studio heads who greenlighted projects. The moguls who had books written about them. Business titans, musical legends, fashionistas, literary icons—we drew them all and we did so by the good graces of one of The Waverly's founding partners, Graydon Carter.

Graydon, the editor in chief of *Vanity Fair*, is one of the most venerable figures in the entire galaxy of print. But The Waverly's popularity was based on more than his illustrious Rolodex. Graydon knew how to throw a party. And everyone wanted to be invited to that party.

We opened at six every evening, and for the first hour or so, we served the minor royalty. Top agents, TV stars, new authors, up-and-coming directors, and sometimes Regis Philbin. The real buzz started around nine, when the main room filled up with Graydon's personal invites. If they graced the cover of *Vanity Fair*, more than likely they graced the red leather banquettes of our dining room. That's when the place really started jumping.

As usual, back in the kitchen, we could not have been more removed from whatever was going on a few feet away. Four cooks had all twelve burners going full blazes and the temperature, even in the dead of winter, ran well over 100 degrees. Waiters could access the narrow pickup and passageways from both the front and back of the galley, so there was a constant chaotic stream of traffic dancing through with balanced plates of meticulously prepared and plated food, clean glasses, dirty glasses, bus tubs full to the brim, all moving along at breakneck pace. The physical distance from the kitchen to the dining room was about twelve feet. The metaphoric distance was slightly further than the moon.

The only connection we had to the high-powered scene out front was the clattering of the printer's dupes coming in. The waitstaff was instructed to note special orders for our VIPs. If Rupert Murdoch wants his chicken extra crispy, there it was in fine blue print on a greasy printout stuck into the lip of the pass. *Murdoch, 210, chick x crisp.* If Ralph or Calvin are entertaining and the whole table decides it must have extra fries immediately, the kitchen knows. I'll see it on the dupe, or my sous chef will note it, or on rare occasion a waiter will run it in the door, especially if we're falling behind. "Four fries on the fly, Chef, please, on 312."

With the caliber of guests we were serving, we had plenty of requests to keep everyone on their toes. Every model on the planet wants the same thing. Sauce on the side, no oil, no butter, no fat. We might as well have served them air. And if it's air they wanted, they would get it. Tim Zagat, the restaurant guide entrepreneur, was the exact opposite. He grabbed me once to pay a compliment to our pork shank, which happened to be as large as a linebacker's thigh. He said, "Chef, I'm a big fella, is that enough for me? I don't want to leave here hungry." And from that day on, I made sure he never did.

The beauty of The Waverly scene was that no matter how much the press frothed at the bit, inside it really was a state of completely controlled but enjoyable chaos. We were an extension of Graydon Carter's living room, and if Graydon liked you, you were invited in. And while this was his party and his restaurant, he rarely complained. Once in a while he'd make a request. "Emil, we need a few lower-priced wines on that wine list." Or, "John, how about a little more goddamned chicken in that chicken potpie." Not quite the plate-throwing pandemonium that the outside world was imagining. Graydon had spent a lifetime getting wined and dined. He knew what worked. He knew what very rich and very famous people liked, and that drove our kitchen mentality.

What I realized quickly was that it was not so difficult to please celebrities. They were so used to being serviced at this ultra-luxurious level that they just expected that their food would be delicious, and prepared exactly the way they liked it. So we fed them. We plied them with nice wines. Then out came the black Amex card. It seemed like an awful lot of our clientele carried it. I assumed it had unimaginable benefits. Fueling your private jet in Cannes. A few nights at the penthouse suite at The Bellagio. Pork shank special at The Waverly. Membership has its privileges. We didn't blink. We just did our jobs.

Eager as I was to keep it low key, though, by merit of my uniform— that simple white jacket with all those buttons—I had become a reluctant minor star of sorts myself. One evening on my ritual dining room catwalk, I felt a tapping on my shoulder. I turned and found myself being summoned by a singer who, in any other venue, would have had a police escort and been fighting off the flashbulbs of the teeming paparazzi. Here, she was just another hungry diner with a megawatt smile enjoying a nice chunk of halibut in a tomato and fennel fumet.

"Hi, I'm Jennie," she says. "I just wanted to tell you, dinner was fabulous."

"Well, thank you, Jennie," I say. "I'm glad you're enjoying it." *Jennie from the block* thinks dinner is delicious. Not Jenny from any block I live on, but who was I to turn down such a nice compliment. Ben Affleck's loss I suppose.

Of course, no matter what we did back in the kitchen, there were always fires to be put out in the front of the house. That's where Emil comes in. He is, like me, an owner, and held the position of general manager. He boasted just the right pedigree to deal with the boldface names. Born in Poland and raised by his French mom, Emil sported a perfect blend of Eastern European socialism and slight French arrogance. His job boiled down to one thing—make sure everyone was having a fabulous time. Any risk of this not happening and Emil was the go-to guy.

The press had gobbled up a story about certain tables existing as the Siberia of The Waverly, but that was media blather for you. We had no Siberia. If you were part of Graydon's party, you were in. Many of the reservations came directly through Graydon's office, and from that information, a grid for the evening was produced—the seating chart. One night Emil was sniffing around the kitchen with me (a good GM always knew what was going on everywhere in his place), when Gwen, the hostess came running in. "Emil. Problem at the door!"

It turned out that a mistake had been made on the grid. We had certain local New York clientele who came from old money. They were the untouchables. These regulars had their favorite wines and favorite foods and favorite place to be seen. It turned out a grievous error had occurred. Scions of two of New York's wealthiest families had been double-booked for the same table. And while one party had already been seated, the other had unwittingly showed up at the door, waiting to be whisked to their spot. Instead, they were left standing amid a sea of babbling agents and models and hangers-on crowding the bar by the door. These are folks who don't wait for anything or anyone. Not good.

Emil was on it. In his charming manner, in a crisp suit—Dolce & Gabbana or perhaps tonight the dark gray Prada, tie as always Hermès—with his suave and slightly unidentifiable accent (he could make it extra French if need be), he had our blue-blooded, double-booked guests seated at a new table before they ever realized they had lost their usual spot. He somehow not only placated them, but convinced them that they had been upgraded, as if we'd rolled out their own personal Concorde.

I watched Emil smiling and making small talk with a new round of guests who had just come in. I could feel the pace picking up. Time to get back to the kitchen. I didn't make it three steps when Lars grabbed my arm. "Chef, do you know Richard Meier?"

Well, not personally of course. I'd not yet plunked down my $5 mil to own a chunk of one of his fabled glass-and-steel buildings—the ones that had helped to redefine Manhattan architecture. "Pleasure to meet you, Mr. Meier," I said to the stately looking gentleman.

He reached beneath his chair and pulled out a dirty plastic bag with the *I heart NY* logo on the side, the kind New Yorkers use to scoop their dog's business with. He handed it to me. It weighed about a ton.

"I grew these in my garden out in East Hampton," he announced. "Can you do something with them?"

I peered into the heavy bag. He had brought me two prize zucchinis that must have weighed about five pounds each. "No problem," I said.

The kitchen was going like a triage scene from an episode of *M\*A\*S\*H*, but I wheedled my way in between two of my cooks. I cleared some cutting board space and sliced the zucchinis first in half, because they really were enormous, and then in half again slicing them into sort of bite-sized triangles. I hit the mise en place and started looking for some inspiration. There was a cold bottle of sparkling water that my runner always gets for me before service begins. Perfect. I pour the water into a mixing bowl and locate a pound of all-purpose flour left over from an experiment from earlier in the afternoon. I add a handful of ice from the oyster station to keep the mixture cold, then I whisk the flour into the carbonated water, all the while dodging the intense kitchen traffic. The last thing these guys need right now is the chef attempting to create on the fly. I dust the little morsels with some flour and drop them into the batter. From the batter they go into the fryer, but not before seven orders of crispy fries get yanked out en route to the dining room. The zucchini goes in for all of about a minute, and at the last second I throw some fresh parsley leaves into the boiling oil.

It crackles brilliantly and turns a shiny dark green. In less than five minutes I return to Richard Meier's table with a platter full of delicate zucchini "tempura." He takes a sample bite, but I can't even wait for his reaction. I hurry back to the kitchen and get food out for ten more tables. When I return to the dining room I see that he has polished off the whole plate.

"Chef," he said, shaking my hand. "I've been growing zucchinis like this for a dozen years, and never once have I cooked one up that tasted like this."

"Mr. Meier," I said. "You can't fry a zucchini and I can't design the Getty Center. I suppose it all evens out in the end."

# The Brothers Calamari

An ominous silence settled over the Margaux dining room following our opening. Still, I was learning a boatload of new skills, even if there were precious few customers to enjoy them. If you'd suggested a mere few years ago during my BFC days that I might end up cooking French food, I'd just as soon have tried out for the Knicks. It was that far out of the realm of my imagination. I was spending a lot of subway time on the way to work memorizing my trusty *Larousse Gastronomique*. I was becoming a fast reader.

Just because we had no diners to speak of, however, didn't mean we could sleep through our days. My job as poissonnier was proving to be an invaluable, though terrifying experience. Under the stressed-out Peter, it was a little like the death march to Bataan, six days a week, fourteen hours a day. Every night he'd order fish from his purveyors, who in turn would go to the famous Fulton Fish Market, which in those days occupied a historic spot along the East River of Manhattan. Forget anything you've heard about famous chefs going down there themselves in their duck boots and L.L. Bean jackets at four a.m. to handle the selection. This, for ninety-nine percent of the chef population, is pure nonsense. In reality, our daily catch arrived by refrigerated panel truck while I was schlepping in on the F train at seven in the morning.

I'd arrive to fresh turbot or wild salmon, bluefin tuna, halibut, octopus from Greece, and branzini from Portugal. When it came to food costs at Margaux, money was no object. The owners had given their top-drawer chef carte blanche to get the best and freshest ingredients available. Despite our lack of business, Peter's arrogance precluded any notion of prudence with his fish budget. Only the very best crossed our polished oak threshold.

Once the Fulton Market delivery guy left his package, we had a fish butcher who devoted his mornings to fending off his hangover and breaking down the fish—filleting all the cuts expertly and saving the bones and heads for stocks, broths, and soups. He was so tanked up some mornings I could barely watch him open his knife bag. Somehow, inexplicably, he never hurt himself or anyone else. Nevertheless, I stayed far away from him. By the time I got busy, all the fish would be laid out neatly in rows on ice in the front of the walk-in fridge, awaiting the execution of whatever Chef dreamed up. I did everything else associated with that piece of fish to get it from inside Peter's head and onto the imported Bernardaud china on the Frette-linen-clad tables in the dining room.

Tonight we had fresh American Red Snapper with Watercress, Hijiki, and Salsify slated for the evening's menu. My first order of business is to pick the watercress of any discolored leaves and cut the stems a few inches from the bottom. Then I soak the hijiki in water to rehydrate. Hijiki, which I had never heard of before working at Margaux, is a dried black seaweed now readily available in supermarkets. Next, I deal with the salsify. This is a tasty and nutritious root vegetable, once cooked, that I had also never worked with before this trial by haute cuisine fire. It's imported from France and resembles half-inch-diameter roots of a tree. There is a black and sticky bark on the outside to be peeled away, uncovering a white and still sticky root that must be plunged in acidulated water (water with some lemon juice) to keep it from oxidizing and turning black. It then must be cooked slowly in a blanc (water with a little white flour) to keep it pristinely white. All of this went on while prepping the other five fish dishes that I was responsible for.

The situation at Margaux, now open for three months, had grown desperate. It wasn't as if we weren't moving *any* meals. We had a handful of regulars, and when the weather was nice, we might get a few walk-ins. But when you spend a small fortune gutting and renovating a place and then hire a staff large enough to run the Palace of Versailles, you have to move more than a few meals. The kitchen staff had settled into a thick malaise born of lack of activity, and Peter was on the prowl, going through some serious shit trying to generate buzz and a little business. Who could blame him?

I was hanging on by a thread, trying to stay focused and pick up anything new while I still had a job, which is not easy when you're staring down thirty pounds of raw cod at seven a.m. before your first espresso. I learned how to lard fish, which requires wielding razor-sharp knives without the benefit of health insurance. First you tackle the basil with your paring knife, creating bullets of the thinly rolled basil. Next you open up surgical-like slits, dozens or more per cod steak, and delicately insert the basil. The slits have to be so thin as to be invisible, and the basil disappears into them. When the fish gets roasted, the basil is dissolved under the high heat, leaving a fragrant, green herbaceous flavor enhanced with a hefty pinch of sea salt and a dollop of extra-virgin. The dish was sensational, but what a pain in the ass. And it left me reeking of fish for days. As poissonnier, I suppose that was a trade hazard.

My mornings were rounded out by a never-ending list of other tasks required for the day's menu. There were sauces to be made, marinades to be whisked, and pounds of potatoes to peel, cook, pass through a tami by hand, and then fold in with copious amounts of butter and cream. You could open a creamery in these mashed potatoes and still Peter would stroll by and stick his finger in the mix and yell, MORE BUTTER! A professional kitchen was not a democracy. More butter it was.

One morning I sliced my finger on a Japanese mandoline, requiring eleven stitches. I waited until *after* the lunch service to visit the emergency room. I came back all bandaged up, and Peter took one look at me and sighed with utter disappointment and disgust. I'm convinced he would have had the same reaction had I returned missing an arm. He had conviction for hard work and an agenda for quality, and I admired him for sticking by it. He was absolutely relentless about his fish and would often send back what seemed like perfectly good snapper just to fuck with the vendor. "Believe me," he once said, "the boat captain himself will start picking out our fish just so he doesn't have to deal with me." I believed him.

Peter had become so obsessed with nailing down that big review that he had us cooking two sets of dinners a night—one for our customers and one for the elusive Bryan Miller, who *still* had not shown his face. On the fateful night when he finally turned up (we were frantically tipped off by our zydeco sommelier), tensions were running high. The *Times* food czar traveled with three other people and they ordered every appetizer on the menu, followed by every entrée—including all four fish dishes on my station. Gary, a kitchen floater, was my partner that night. He was a recently born-again Christian who on more than one occasion asked me to "watch my language." My corrupted soul was the last thing on my mind as the Miller order came in.

We decided that I would pick up three of the dishes and Gary would cook and plate the fourth, a ridiculously simple grilled wild Alaskan salmon. I tackled the turbot with leeks, sautéed Dover sole with a citrus beurre monte, and the branzini with Russian fingerlings sliced razor thin with an olive tapenade. In no time at all, my plates were in the pass, perfectly cooked and waiting to be picked up by the waiters and whisked to Miller's table. So were a rack of lamb, foie gras, and two different veal dishes and all of the sides. All that was missing was a simple plate of wild salmon. Somehow, Christian Gary had forgotten to fire the one dish he was responsible for. So now all of the piping warm, meticulously plated dishes were waiting for the salmon, which had just hit the grill.

All seven cooks behind the line were silent with anticipation and horror, watching this dude finally put the last plate up in the window. It was so quiet you could almost hear the gas flowing through the jets on the Wolf stoves.

Peter stepped into the pass, took one look at me—it was my station after all—and then surveyed the lineup of plates. He lifted his arm parallel to the floor and walked the entire length of the cooking line, sliding one Bernardaud plate after another off the stainless-steel shelf and onto the tiled floor with a splendid crash. The popping explosions of expensive china sounded like firecrackers on the Fourth of July. The seven cooks stared in awe as I stood there silently calculating my unemployment benefits. "Again!" he screamed. "Make it again. Now!" And make it again we did. All twelve dishes, from scratch.

Ten minutes later, twelve new plates lined the pass. Peter gave a quick inspection and a nod. The waiters grabbed them and, tracking through four inches of broken china, sticky reduced sauces, and squished food, made a sterling presentation to Señor Miller and his table.

By eleven p.m. the porters were sweeping, mopping, and shoveling up the culinary carnage. The last seating had taken place and more money had been lost. Bryan Miller and his mighty Parker sword had marched off into the night. I hightailed it to the locker room to peel out of my fish blood–drenched sweaty chef whites. Riding home on the F train fifteen minutes later, I noticed no one took a seat anywhere near me. Ahhh, the heady aroma of day-old fish.

Margaux's glowing three-star *New York Times* review materialized several months too late to stem the tide. By then the owners had strong-armed Peter into downgrading our menu from poached, line-caught halibut to a fried calamari appetizer, and "maybe a little rigatoni with some red sauce."

"C'mon, Chef, whaddya think? People love that stuff. Would that be so terrible?" I overheard one of the brothers ask. I thought Peter might have an embolism. It was not looking good. The vendors at this point had all gone C.O.D. They certainly didn't want to become partners in a struggling enterprise, although most of them already had, by virtue of their unpaid accounts receivables with Margaux.

If my second bounced paycheck hadn't convinced me to jump ship, the final nail in the coffin came when Peter vented his frustration one night by jabbing a wicked-hot sauté pan into my forearm. "Fucking ouch!" I shouted. That actually made him smile for a second. Not much did at that point. Certainly not the calamari idea. I had a sneaking suspicion my contribution to the world of French cooking had run its course.

# Waltz for PJ

Despite the fact I had nothing new lined up, it was a relief to be paroled from Margaux. I felt so beaten down by the experience that I even wondered whether I wanted to do this job anymore. It was clear I needed a change of scenery, and Gina agreed to steal a couple of days off to share in my misery. We hightailed it down to South Beach to decompress and regroup. Somehow I thought a few days with my wife would be exactly the ticket. I couldn't have been more wrong.

We sat on the beach in stony silence, soaking up the rays, watching the beautiful, much-happier-than-us people rollerblade by, sipping dispiritedly on our overly cheerful-looking tropical drinks. There isn't a more pathetic thing in life than a frozen cocktail with a colorful parasol poking out in your face when you feel about as festive as sunburn. It was the first time Gina and I had been alone together in ages and suddenly we had nothing to say. When did this happen? Was she starting to lose interest in me? Or had my habitual career whining and negativity finally taken its toll. Self-doubt, seasoned with a healthy dose of insecurity, drifted in like the tide.

\* \* \*

A few days later I was back in our apartment, alone in the middle of the morning, which after a few years on a cook's schedule felt as foreign to me as if I had landed on the Upper East Side. I spent my time idly circling classifieds in the *New York Times* with a felt-tipped pen, waiting for the next big thing to leap out at me.

The call came from a guy named PJ, a super-talented line cook whom I had befriended at Yellowfingers. PJ had worked one day a week with me for the extra cash, when he wasn't at his other gig under André Soltner at Lutèce, which was not a bad place to be if you were looking to be upwardly mobile. Soltner was about to cash out and PJ had decided to go out on his own. So when a jazz fanatic, impresario, and one-time food broker named Neil got it in his craw that New York needed a new jazz supper club, he took space in an abandoned Stanford White–designed hotel called the Wolcott. The boarded-up edifice, which featured a golden-age ballroom, was plunked down in the no-man's-land of the West 30s. Neil had a vision of turning it into a high-style cabaret and eatery from an era long gone by. PJ got together with Neil probably over about a hundred beers at three in the morning armed with a Bic Rolling Writer and a crumpled cocktail napkin. Throw in Neil's family money, a stack of credit cards, and PJ's skill as a cook, and The Five Spot was born.

What are the three most important aspects of any retail enterprise? Location, location, and location. The Five Spot had none out of three. That didn't deter Neil or his investors, a motley crew of career bartenders, general contractors, music bookers, and a few other hangers-on. Somewhere in this formerly opulent, rococo dust bowl of a hotel, he had a vision to bring back a small slice of New York from a jazzier day and age. Of course, any sane person might ask where the logic was. Take an old hotel ballroom, a war zone of a neighborhood, and add a genre of music that absolutely no one outside of Paris wants to pay to see or hear, season with some upscale food, and you have the perfect recipe for disaster. When do I start?

The Five Spot's entrance was nestled between the locked steel roll-door gates of a shady Chinese knickknack shop and a counterfeit Nike sneaker emporium. You could just feel the glamour oozing from the place. Once again I found myself reporting on my first day of work to a hail of nail guns, power saws, spackle tape, and gold leaf application. Somewhere amid the dated wreckage you could see what the ownership had in mind. The place had twenty-four-foot ceilings, balconies lining the place, a six-foot raised stage, and a proscenium arch. With a lot of work it could be restored to its original splendor.

As the construction came along, it was clear that they were shooting for the moon. Elegant linens adorned the tables and I saw the familiar crates of Bernardaud china and baroque silverware fit for a pharaoh's dinner, arriving by panel truck. PJ, all six-foot-four of him without his nine-inch toque, tried to keep up his end in the kitchen. He took advantage of his André Soltner training and my goodwill (unemployment will do that to you) and designed a French-inspired brasserie menu. Perhaps a Tarte Alsace or some choucroute with your Bud Light, sir?

I was assigned the position of tournet, which in the French system meant that I'd be revolving from station to station nightly. PJ was playing his cards smart so that when the inevitable "Chef, tomorrow I go back to my country for three months" speech gets made by your most loyal and dependable south-of-the-border line cook, he was covered. I was glad to be on board. PJ was a decent guy and this was his first big test. He could count on me to deliver a solid, reliable job. However, there were distractions. It was a jazz place, after all.

While we were testing recipes one afternoon, an amazing sound filtered through the din of the kitchen. Bobby Lyle, a prolific jazz pianist, was onstage warming up on a twelve-foot Steinway grand piano that had been brought in by crane. No one else even noticed, but I needed to check this out. I stole away for a break and stood there watching and listening. Lyle hit a low bass note and its booming resonance nearly brought the beams down on the place. I had never heard an instrument like that so up close and personal. Lyle noticed me watching. "Can I help you, son?" he asked.

"Can you play 'Waltz for Debbie'?" It just all of a sudden seemed more important than anything that was going on back in the kitchen.

Bobby Lyle stared at me for a moment. "Waltz for Debbie" is a classic, beautifully written standard by Bill Evans, a tragic genius pianist who died way too young. My father used to play it. Finally, Bobby said, "Have a seat, young man."

I sat there rapt while he played the most breathtaking rendition for an audience of one, or so I thought. When it was over, all the carpenters and painters in the room started applauding. At that moment PJ stuck his head out of the kitchen, wondering what the fuss was about. He impatiently motioned me back inside, where a boom box was blasting some twenty-minute meandering live performance by the Grateful Dead. *Quel horreur!*

We opened on New Year's Eve of 1992 with David Sanborn, the prolific multi–Grammy Award winning alto saxophonist as the featured act. He was a serious name who had played with everyone from James Taylor to Stevie Wonder to Roger Daltry of The Who. We were sold out and had a line stretching out the door and down West 31st Street. There were publicists and music people and crowd control. We had 250 filled seats and the kitchen was a madhouse, a complete assault. With a big act like David Sanborn coming on, everyone wanted to be fed fast and at once. But believe me, it was not the French specialties they were clamoring for. The printer was spewing out orders for skewers and burgers and steaks and more burgers. I was slapping them out as fast as they could be plated. It was insanity for roughly sixty minutes, and then it just stopped cold in its tracks. Sanborn came on. He played his set. The audience applauded and then went home. And that's the way it was from day one. No one ordered the choucroute, the moules, the Tarte Alsace. We couldn't give away the saucissons et verts. Not only had the French dream died in childbirth, but the place was running deeply in the red and Neil was despondent. He walked over to PJ one morning not long after we opened and said, "Hey, could you make me a sandwich? Something light because I'd like to have a little food before I go upstairs and jump out the window."

I'm sure it must have been disappointing for PJ, too. This was his first gig, his debut, and the only thing on his menu anyone would touch was the equivalent of chicken fingers. I felt his pain. On the other hand, in the hours during prep time, there was music going on just beyond my earshot. And it was hard for me to ignore.

One afternoon I was grinding twenty-five pounds of fresh sirloin with shallots and parsley for the usual run of overthought "chef-ed up" burgers, when I heard and felt what I thought at first was thunder. I snuck out the kitchen door, and there up on stage was the drummer Dennis Chambers of the Brecker Brothers band. Dennis was the original drummer for the revolutionary seventies funk band Parliament. He had so many drums in his kit that I wondered where the other musicians were going to stand. He had tom-toms and cymbals, two bass drums and, behind him, a gigantic gong. I stared in disbelief at what I was hearing. He played so forcefully, joyously, and loud that the rim shot from his snare drum nearly cut me in half. I lost half an hour of prep time just staring, mesmerized, with a huge smile across my face.

The Five Spot boasted a seven-night-a-week jazz schedule to compete with any of the best venues downtown. I would have happily worked for free just to see and hear some of the music we were booking. As far as my cooking career, we weren't doing anything magical in the kitchen, but PJ had amassed a very good and colorful staff. Gerard, the European-trained pastry chef, was a friendly and talented former skinhead from Wembley, UK, covered in skull tattoos and painful-looking, calculated piercings. This fearsome-looking guy would craft the most beautiful and delicious chocolate genoise cake, whipping egg yolks into a frenzy, and his petits fours were as tiny and delicate as flowers. The second he was off duty, Gerry could be found in an East Village dive bar whacking some guy across the face with a two-by-four just for kicks. He'd show up at work the next day scratched and bloodied, cut up, black and blue, and get started on those petits fours again. One day he pulled an uncharacteristic no-show. When three days passed, we grew concerned. We finally tracked down a friend of his who went over to his apartment to explore. As it turned out, Gerry had met a woman at one of his favorite haunts and took her back to his place, where she handcuffed him to the radiator. She left him locked up, took his cash and split. The friend called for help, got Gerry hacksawed free, and he was on time for his next shift two hours later. The Valrhona Genoise was safe.

There were others: Keith, the expert at the art of charcuterie—because what jazz fan who took the LIRR in to Penn Station hoping to hear Kenny G wasn't hungry for country pâté with cornichons and Dijon? After a few weeks, even the ravenous staff got sick of eating it for the family meal. Keith was the first to go. The gelatin gravy train had derailed.

I struck up a personal friendship with Habibi from Egypt—a one-man culinary special forces unit. He would fire up three rigatoni marinara, two roast chickens, and one of PJ's overly complicated, overthought fish preparations, with searing water streaming down his reddened, scarred arms as he plated half a dozen dishes by himself, all the while chewing a ubiquitous hunk of hashish. He was a fast-and-furious line cook, impervious to pain. He once removed a pomme soufflé boiling in the fryer at full tilt with the tips of his bare fingers. I wouldn't have believed it myself if I wasn't standing right there.

I was having fun with these guys and bringing in something that resembled a paycheck and catching some interesting music on the side, as well. It offered a great smoke screen to the painful reality that Gina and I were adrift. Or more accurately, I was adrift. Her career was taking off and she was making new friends who actually had jobs that allowed them to go out at night, as opposed to, let's say, her husband. We might have been bickering if we ever saw each other enough to bother, so maybe I shouldn't have been so surprised about Jenna.

It started the same as it does for any man in relationship trouble. Jenna was an aspiring actress with incredible green eyes and an innocence that made me wonder, can she possibly be for real? I should have known better. I didn't have that first drink with Jenna to step out on Gina. She offered a soothing shoulder for my troubled mind, and way back then, her acting aspirations seemed original and heartfelt to me. She was pursuing a dream, and how could I not dig that? I gave her confidence and she gave me the attention that Gina had finally and understandably given up on providing.

Jenna worked the front door at The Five Spot, taking phone calls, making reservations, putting out fires, and making herself generally useful. She was a struggling artist who got to eat for free and see these big acts that everyone else on the staff could care less about. One afternoon in the kitchen we were doing some kind of highbrow variation of a mother sauce that no one was going to order, with a load of veal bones, tomatoes, garlic, and a stock that needed reducing and straining. Every pot in the place was in use and PJ hollered out for me to get one out of storage. I scoured the kitchen and told him we were out. "Have Jenna get it," he yelled.

It had been a long morning. I don't smoke cigarettes, and all of Habibi's arm-twisting had not turned me into a hash addict. I decided a Jenna fix would be just the thing. I went out to the front station to have a quick flirt. The look she gave me when I asked about the pot nearly made me run back to the kitchen in terror. "C'mon," she said. "I'll unlock the storeroom."

I followed her up a little-used set of stairs to an alcove above the balcony that I didn't even know existed. She unlocked an industrial strength Master lock and let us in. I rummaged about the shelves until I found the pot PJ needed. Jenna stood there staring at me. I looked at her. Then I planted a kiss squarely on her mouth, right there in that dusty storage room. Before she had a chance to react or even say a word, I grabbed the pot and walked out.

# Reluctant Patty

We were cooking some very satisfying food at The Waverly. Simple, high-end dishes that our regular customers kept coming back for again and again. I'm a great proponent of going with what works. I'd once been on a scouting trip to Capri, Italy, and I'd read in a culinary guidebook about a trattoria serving the sweetest, freshest seafood in the region. Of course I had to check the place out.

The moment I walked in I felt like I had been there before. The décor, the fancy linen on the tabletops, the doorway that was so reminiscent of an old speakeasy. Even the menu items seemed as if I'd sampled them before as a kid growing up. An old woman who could have been the twin sister of my grandmother brought me a plate of risotto with artichokes, plain and simple as can be, and something called pesce alla mediterranea: baked fish with potatoes, oregano, and chilies. Sure enough, it lived up to the guidebook's glowing reviews. As I enjoyed my leisurely meal, I pulled out my tattered twenty-five-year-old guidebook and found the page that had led me here in the first place. I realized what my sense of déjà vu was about. The restaurant had not changed a bit in two decades, right down to the paintings on the walls.

Here, in an ancient town in Italy, they did things slowly and methodically, without fanfare. No food stacked on the plate piled to the
ceiling, requiring a set of architectural tools to deconstruct it. No
lengthy descriptions on the menu of how the calf had been gently raised
by nuns on a hillside with imported grasses. It was just about the food.
After a strong espresso and delicious biscotti, I packed up my twenty-
five-year-old book and realized some things never change, and never
should.

I returned to New York and The Waverly with an invigorated sense of
tradition. That's not to say I wasn't willing to experiment. New York
may be one of the great seasonal marketplaces on the planet. If it grows,
swims, oinks, bleats, or moos, and can be had within a hundred miles
of the city, I'm in. We purchase from upstate farms, Long Island farms,
and the Hudson Valley, which, in addition to its superb produce, is
known for its game farms as well as its orchards. This attention to local
producers is all part of what we do, which is provide the freshest, finest, and most local foods for dishes that appeal to arguably the tough-
est audience in the world. New Yorkers love food and they know what
they want. This meant that I was on a constant mission to design dishes
that were as recognizable as they were simple. We even kowtowed to
our vegan audience, coming up with a quinoa dish, based on a grain
that was originally discovered by the Incas and, according to ancient
legend, was the perfect food. Eat it and you will no doubt live forever. I
experimented cooking it almost like a risotto; toasting it in a pan with a
little shallot and olive oil. You deglaze with some white wine and then
add stock made from root vegetables, simmering the concoction until it
becomes tender to the bite. Of course, this dish pleased our eco-centric
customers: the potting-soil-under-their-manicure actresses and rock
stars on their twelfth step. We aimed to please a lot of the people all of

the time, but that was not always possible. Customers can be very finicky and they seem to always be at their very worst when we are going through the roof.

It's 8:30 on a Thursday, our busiest night, and it's Fashion Week, the week when the most important international designers descend upon New York to show their coming season's collections. The models and designers and accompanying attendants spend their day preening in a gigantic tent set up in Bryant Park in midtown, as the city plays host to a carnival of high couture. With all of that fashion energy percolating, you end up with a lot of personalities to be fed. We're running full blast in the back when a dupe comes in from a famous household-name designer who wants a mushroom omelet. Easy enough, one would think. Except we don't serve breakfast, we don't serve brunch, and we have no omelet pans. I grab my most trusted runner, Jesus, and tell him to check downstairs in storage and find me either a nonstick sauté pan or a brand-new regular sauté pan. Jesus stands with me side by side every night in the heat of the battle, clearing tables, filling waters, bringing up clean napkins, and making sure guests who have ordered steak get the proper silverware. How many times have you ordered soup in a restaurant only to have to flag down a waiter to get you a spoon? Thanks to Jesus and the rest of this hardworking staff, this almost never happens here.

He returns from the basement storage room several minutes later and reports that we have no new pans and no nonstick pans either. Great. Meanwhile, the stainless-steel shelves above the cooking line, where I expedite and watch and taste every dish before it exits the kitchen, are crammed with finished plates awaiting delivery to the dining room. Consistency is a challenge in a high-volume restaurant, and it's paramount that the first chicken to leave the kitchen tastes exactly the same as the fiftieth. The only way to achieve this is to keep dozens of clean spoons handy and taste a little sauce here and a little vegetable garnish there. You use five senses on this job, sometimes even six.

While I'm trying to juggle fifty things and the omelet situation, Garret, our newest waitstaff hire, walks into the kitchen a hair too quickly and nearly collides with Luiz, who is polishing and restocking glasses for the bar. Garret holds a half-eaten plate of Dover sole that a customer has complained has "too many bones."

"Really?" I ask, exasperated. "How many does she think it is supposed to have?" Jesus grabs the plated fish and begins to fillet it before Garret even figures out what is going on. Meanwhile, Omelet Guy's waiter wants to know how breakfast is coming. I grab the newest-looking sauté pan I can find out of a stack of about twenty on the shelf, go around to the range, and put the empty pan on the flame full blast. I empty half a pound of salt in and after a moment or two, toss the whole thing into the oven. This will "cure" the pan, sealing the pores of the metal and making it as good as nonstick. The designer's appetizers left the kitchen a while ago, which means I have maybe a five-minute window to prepare the pan and then cook an omelet in order for all the food to hit the table at the same time.

I run down to the basement with a stainless-steel bowl, grab three farm fresh brown eggs from the walk-in fridge, and crack them into the bowl on my way up the stairs. I hand the broken shells to a runner as I grab a dinner fork from the waiters' station and start to beat the eggs right then and there. I dodge around the bustling cook line, grabbing herbs and a handful of chanterelle mushrooms that had already been sautéed with leeks for a special this evening. I add some cheddar cheese as I reach into the oven and grab the blazing hot sauté pan, trying to ignore the pain. The shelves are overflowing with plates, five of which are now waiting to go to the designer's table. I dump the salt from my newly treated pan, pour a drop of canola oil in, and rub vigorously with a kitchen towel. Ready.

The pan is still blistering hot, so in preparation for the eggs I use clarified butter, that is, butter that has had all of its milk solids removed so it can reach a higher smoke point and not burn. We always have it on hand for situations like this, as well as to make the hollandaise for the Dover sole. I pour the eggs in the hot pan and proceed to Omelet Making 101. As I execute the final flip, the cheese starts to melt sumptuously. All the other plates are up in the window now. The timing is perfect and totally by chance.

One more turn to go this evening. We have seated and served the entire dining room and we're about to do it all over again. Garret, who seems to be inheriting all the troubles tonight, arrives in the kitchen. "What now, brother?" I inquire curtly.

"The lady who ordered the gazpacho garnished with crab is allergic to shellfish."

"What the fuck, dude. How does she read 'crab' on the menu, order it, and then send it back?" You really got to wonder sometimes.

"*Una sopa, no cangrejo, RÁPIDO!*" I yell to the pantry station, thinking I will get the soup faster if I ask for it in my hacked-up Spanish. Jesus is not only the lead runner, but also diplomat and interpreter for our predominantly Mexican staff. When there are raises to discuss or discipline needs to be dished out, Jesus is there to make sure I am understood. We have a good working relationship, and I know if I have to ream someone out, there is no judgment on his part, even if it's him getting the reaming. The crab soup, sans crab, goes out. Monsieur Designer has his omelet. Half of Fashion Week seems to be lined up out the door. No doubt we have not heard the last of the ridiculous requests.

Managing the tastes of a fickle public comes with the territory. However, I have to confess, the day Graydon announced that he thought we needed a good rare burger on the menu, I paused. It never crossed my mind that a burger was just the thing we needed. In my line of work you hope to make your mark with something a little more distinguished than a patty of ground chuck. Other high-end places had run amok inventing their take on the all-American classic. Fellow chefs were spinning out burgers with buffalo and veal and pork and short ribs. They were mixing in every herb ever grown—chopped laurel, savory, sorrel, lavender, parsley, chives, rosemary, and thyme. It was like a Simon & Garfunkel song topped with specialty artisanal cheeses: Stilton imported from Great Britain, handmade mozzarella from Joe's in Little Italy, French Camembert foam, fondue sauce that required its own cook just to service one burger. All of this on a brioche sesame seed Vidalia onion roll made with spring water from a lake near Geneva. I created my own admittedly prosaic take.

I scored twenty pounds of good ol' American chuck, the kind I ate growing up, except now I got it from an all-natural, hormone-free supplier. Twenty percent fat content, because what is a good burger unless you bite into it and have those tasty juices running down your chin. You mix it by hand, but not too much, lest you emulsify the fat and protein, which has a tendency to make it tough and dry. Paint a little olive oil on both sides with a pastry brush and season with some kosher salt and fresh ground pepper. Sear it hot on the grill, flipping only once to get those nice score marks on the meat.

For the buns, I must have sampled every bakery in New York. I tried sesame, whole wheat, Kaiser, and even challah. I experimented with sourdough onion, not to mention Thomas's and other premium English muffins, but nothing seemed just right. There was too much thinking going on here. Ultimately what I wanted was a bun that was soft enough to the bite that you could get your mouth into it but not have it fall apart from all the juicy goodness. I walked over to the neighborhood supermarket and bought every commercially available roll I could find—the ones with all the chemicals that keep it fresh longer than a Hostess Twinkie. Score! I won't give away my favorite brand (it was the one with the least amount of chemicals in it), but when I rolled it out for its first tasting, the partners went bananas. There was no way out.

The Waverly Burger was born, with fries and no extra charge for the cheese.

The critics loved it. Our customers loved it. Even the mayor loved it. The lowly burger, which I thought (or secretly hoped) had little or no business on our menu, was voted Best High-End Burger in New York by *Time Out* magazine. So much for my theory. No matter how many times we raised the price, they kept coming back for more. I love burgers.

# Running from Stilettos

From one ill-advised storage-room kiss, I became a cliché, along with several other new titles to my credit that either my wife or girlfriend would use on me before it was all over. Cheating bastard. Shithead. Liar. Prick. Did I mention asshole? Pick one. My life had become a comic farce, a hellish game of grown-up dodgeball. I was avoiding Gina at home and ducking Jenna at work. Lying to Gina was easier to rationalize. I was sleeping with another woman for chrissakes. There wasn't a lot of gray here. No one would ever accuse me of confronting problems straightaway, so no surprise, I was going to avoid the domestic drama as long as possible.

But avoiding Jenna? She rightly considered herself the hot new thing in my life and she wanted attention. And she got it. Sex with a much younger woman who is not your wife is a real ego boost at first. But by week two it starts to feel pretty complicated. And a month into it, you find yourself unfairly blaming the whole sordid affair on some slight your wife surely never perpetrated. All you can think is, this has got to stop. But by that point, it has become an addiction.

I had become so addicted to the good parts that I tended to overlook the less desirable parts. Like having to go to parties full of struggling young actresses, or what's worse, struggling young actresses' boyfriends, talking about their "craft." Have you seen *Raging Bull*? I asked one emerging young talent.

"Ummm, ohhhh, yes. Of course. Pacino was amazing in that. I'll have to rent the DVD again."

Abject torture, but it was the price you paid for the rest. And all set to the backdrop of some thumping new CD of an inane band that was fabulously musical to the postcollege demographic and completely unlistenable to me. Add in my sinking embarrassment the time when Jenna had to kick her roommate out while she was studying for an exam so we could have a little privacy. It all was wrong, and how could I possibly rationalize my inexcusable behavior, except that I played in the high school band and everyone knows that the band guy never got the cheerleader.

Somehow, thanks to this whole cooking thing, the cheerleader's interest had been piqued. It was mystifying and completely superficial, but all the same, cooking had given me confidence in a way that nothing else had. Formerly unattainable, attractive women now showered me with interest. What the hell was I supposed to do? Maybe it had something to do with that double-breasted starched white chef's coat, with all those cotton buttons. Very militaristic, and you know the saying about women being a sucker for a man in uniform. Suffice it to say, I was having one tough time letting go.

Fortunately, I still had a job at The Five Spot to keep me occupied. That, along with the fact that I had to stave off the Jenna problem while at work, kept me busy desperately trying to stay out of trouble. Clearly it was time to move on.

Abdul, our Pakistani food runner and the most polite guy on earth, inexplicably had been handed the job of general manager. He was so polite and soft-spoken that he may have actually turned it down, but probably no one heard him while they were handing him the keys. It didn't really matter because our jazz schedule got cut back from seven headliners a week to five so-so acts, to two nights if management even opted to fork out the paltry booking fee for the low-rent acts we had resorted to. There was hardly anyone left for Abdul to manage. The only French thing left on the menu was fries, and my cooking expertise had been reduced to well-done burgers for a bridge-and-tunnel crowd that was a lot more interested in the theme parties the owners would throw in desperation than any food or jazz we could serve up. One night, a patron got refused entrance to one of our new bashes because he looked crazy. He returned from his car wielding a machete. We'd come a long way from "Waltz for Debbie."

Ironically, my ticket out came in the guise of a phone call from Gina. One of her hair clients happened to be Bobby Flay, whose Mesa Grill and Bolo were packed and ringing up critical acclaim. He had written several cookbooks and made a name for himself on the Food Network. Bobby was popular and successful and because of that, many chefs talked a lot of shit about him. There is rarely genuine respect among fellow chefs. If anything, we are a jealous and covetous lot. Still, for all the grief that Bobby was getting for his fame, he was unfazed and impressed me as a down-to-earth, hardworking New York guy. I had met him once at Margaux when he'd strolled into the kitchen to check out the digs. I didn't know at first what to make of him. Fancy suit, expensive haircut, not what I expected, but he was friendly and sincere.

"What's up?" I asked Gina, wondering why this unusual call in the middle of my day and starting to break a sweat.

"Bobby's got a friend looking for someone to cook in the Hamptons," she said, relieving *that* anxiety at least. He said he'd put in a good word for you. She told me the name of the chic East Hampton eatery. Did I want in?

I thought about it. Sweltering all summer in the city versus days off at the beach? Slinging burgers at a jazz joint that no longer had jazz versus testing my chops at what I'd been told was probably the hottest restaurant on the East Coast, from Memorial Day to Labor Day? Plus 154 nautical miles distance between me and the Island of Manhattan? Surely that would be enough space to breathe some fresh sea air and unravel the romantic mess that I had gotten myself tangled up in.

Of course there were issues. Where would I live? What would happen after the summer when the gig ran out? Would Gina even be able to spend any time out on the East End of Long Island, or was I just making matters worse? Clearly we were going to have to talk. And then there was Jenna. We were going to have to talk, too. And it was going to be the exact same talk. I had this fantasy. Why not just sit down with both of them together, come clean, and sort the whole thing out reasonably. Gina could say her piece, Jenna hers, and then we could all come to an amicable solution. It was a full-blown hallucination induced by the distress of hurting someone I cared for very deeply. It was time to get my shit together. For everyone involved.

I told PJ the next morning that I was going to be moving on. He was hardly surprised, and in fact I suspect he was relieved he wouldn't have to let me go. Whoever hadn't been axed was looking for work. No doubt PJ had his poker in all sorts of fires, too. I changed into my chef's whites and started my shift.

I should have known better than to tell anyone on the job about my plans if I had any interest in breaking the news of my departure gently to Jenna. I was minding my own business, firing up the handful of orders that had come in when I heard the unmistakable *click click click* of stiletto heels on the tiled floor. I looked up and there were those legs, all five-foot-nine of them, slicing menacingly toward me in a short, pleated miniskirt. Jenna stopped squarely in front of PJ, glaring at me, hands on her hips, hyperventilating. PJ stared at her, speechless himself because there was no reason in the world for his hostess to be standing in his kitchen. He had been raised at Lutèce, where no woman in stilettos had probably ever set foot in thirty years. I couldn't tell who was hyperventilating more, PJ or Jenna. Me, I just stood there watching this standoff, wondering who would break first. Jenna took the honors.

"You asshole, you motherfucker, you piece of shit." She didn't miss a beat, going on for a good sixty seconds about all the various ways I had wrecked her life. When she was done, she heaved a greasy brown paper bag at me. It broke, scattering its contents all over the floor. Jenna was a health nut and she had brought me a sack of dried fruits and nuts and grains, which at least helped me with my daily fiber intake throughout the duration of our tryst. She turned and stormed off, every last member of the kitchen admiring her delightful pleated skirt and its curvy contents as she made her dramatic exit stage left. The laughter and applause from the kitchen staff was deafening. Her performance would have garnered a standing ovation if everyone wasn't already standing.

# Angst Hampton

Nick & Toni's existed out in the fabled real estate of the East End of Long Island known as "The Hamptons," a long skinny strip of pristine beaches, fabulous mansions, country-chic little villages, and shiny exotic automobiles. I had grown up all of forty-five minutes from East Hampton, where I found myself limping the old Mazda past my former stomping grounds and out for my job interview. Most New Yorkers have this myopic view of Long Island. There's Kennedy Airport, Jones Beach, and then the Hamptons. The three million of us who live in between do not get a lot of recognition. And truth be told, I had never warmed up to the superhot social scene out on the East End when I was younger. It felt removed and otherworldly, as if it existed for someone else. Now I was diving headfirst into it. By the time traffic eased, the normally two-hour drive had stretched to four and I was lost in the village and too embarrassed to ask for directions. I finally found the place and angled into a space out front. My car mercifully wheezed to a grinding halt.

The restaurant was located in a pretty, old two-story house on the picturesque main street in East Hampton. It had a welcoming farmhouse look to its exterior. The main room was lined with cozy tables covered with white linen and simple dishware accented with a tasteful floral accent. The space featured a prominent wood-burning pizza oven that a cook was in the process of stoking when I walked in. The scent of the fire and orange hue of the flame set a lovely ambience, a delectable smoky aroma wafting over the hundred or so not too tightly packed seats. I asked where I might find the chef, and the guy on the fire pointed toward the kitchen. From the moment I walked in, I was struck by a sense of calm about the place. I was no longer in the city.

Chef Ted was a sweet, even-tempered guy who had trained at La Varenne in Paris. He greeted me with a warm handshake, dropping everything to get us both espressos. I was digging the country life already and the buzz of the Long Island Expressway was fading fast. Ted asked me the requisite questions and we talked for nearly an hour over espressos and biscotti. The founder and owner, Jeff Salaway, stopped by and we spoke pleasantly for several moments. What a civilized way to spend an afternoon.

Ted offered me the job of sous chef, his number two. My shaky connection to Bobby Flay had landed me this bump up the ladder. That, and some very fortunate timing. Nick & Toni's, like the rest of the Hamptons hot spots, had to ramp up its staff big-time for the impending crush. The summer population of the town increases tenfold from Memorial Day to Labor Day. A year's worth of business had to take place in three short months. Every season back in the city there were at least a few cooks working their way up the culinary food chain who happened to be buried in a bad job, a bad relationship, or both—and desperate enough to move to Long Island, double their monthly income, and take a temporary job. I fit the bill perfectly.

This was to be my first foray into a kitchen management role. While I was positive I was less than qualified for the job, it was a small place and the position was more glorified cook than manager. I figured I could at least cook my way out of any embarrassing situations.

Now that I had agreed to take this gigantic step, I had to take care of a few logistics. Like where to live. As luck would have it, Ted's girl-friend Lynn, a waitress, had a room for rent at her place in Noyack, a small local fishing town stuck out on the bay near Sag Harbor. Ted made a call and five minutes later I was driving twenty minutes away to check it out. The house turned out to be a lovely, one-hundred-year-old Cape set back from the main road overlooking a creek in the back-yard and deep woods creeping up on the property. I felt nervous already. There were trees involved. My wildlife experience was mostly limited to farm-raised rabbits neatly packaged in airtight Cryovac packaging. I was hardly the country-boy type. Like Woody Allen, I was at "two with nature." But this was the gig, so I went with it. I'd have a single bed, a dresser, and a row of windows staring off the back of the house at what-ever wildlife existed beyond in those deep, insect-infested woods.

There were two other women in the house, each renting a bedroom. My share would be one-third the rent, which seemed doable with the raise in pay Ted had offered me. The gravity of this life change was starting to sink in. Despite the fact that this had all been Gina's idea, I wasn't sure she understood the ramifications. Or maybe she did. Either way, confronting my deep sense of marital unease was precisely why I was sitting in a bare bedroom contemplating my life in the middle of the woods in the first place. It was time to buck up and get on with it. I drove back to the restaurant, accepted Ted's offer, and hit the LIE for the long drive home.

Gina, who had been hinting for months that she was sick of living in Brooklyn, took it all in stride and decided that the time had come for us to return to the real world. Translation? Downtown Manhattan. In just a matter of a few phone calls we gave up Uncle Vinny's railroad flat and Gina secured temporary residence with one of her stylist colleagues. Living all summer on her gay best friend's couch was probably not her idea of paradise, but she liked the idea of weekends in the Hamptons. She was a lot more flexible than me, and because of her line of work, better suited to the East End lifestyle than I was. Whatever apprehensions I might be having, Gina was ready to make it a fabulous summer.

A week later I found myself back in East Hampton, rummaging through my backpack filled with underwear and T-shirts, searching for my knife kit. I was staring at a forty-pound box of whole Berkshire pork loins, teetering on a good old-fashioned panic attack. What had I gotten myself into this time? I hadn't been in the door long enough to button my chef's coat when Ted called out, "Hey Johnny, can you break down these pork loins for me?" The larger restaurants in the city where I had worked always had a full-time butcher on staff. This makes for more consistent portions and far less waste. Butchering is, after all, an art form. One I had never bothered to learn. Unfortunately I couldn't just say, "Ahh sorry, Chef, I don't know how to do that." I mean he just hired me to be the sous chef, for fuck's sake. So I yelled out, "GOT IT."

I took the pork loins out of the box. These were not nice prepackaged pork loins like you see in the store. A whole loin of pork is a massive, distended thing full of rib bones and cartilage and fat. Out of the corner of my eye I saw another guy, Joe, who I recalled was just starting as well. He stood about six-foot-two, 250 pounds, and resembled a teddy bear, the kind of guy most women would feel very safe having around. He reminded me of my uncle Leo, a New York City cop for twenty years, and my aunt would always tell us how safe *she* felt when he was around. Of course, Uncle Leo carried a .38, so that might have had something to do with it.

I started in on the beast, and butcher it I did, in the worst possible sense. In about two seconds my cutting board was like a bloodbath. I was thinking about throwing the whole mess in the garbage and looking into dishwashing opportunities when Joe's eyes met mine from across the kitchen. He knew I was in trouble. He walked over calm as can be, got out his boning knife and took me through the whole process step by step. He showed me the way to stand over the thing, the angle at which you attack it. He patiently demonstrated how you start on the thinner end so if you are cutting chops you can cut the smallest one thicker so that they all come out the same weight. Apparently he had worked in a butcher shop in Queens during high school, so this had become second nature for him.

Without making a fuss, Joe got me through all ten loins no problem. For the rest of that night, we worked side by side on the hot line. He worked the pasta station and I worked the middle, roasting quails and fillets of wild striped bass, while sautéing sides of broccoli rabe with paper-thin slivers of garlic and fruity extra-virgin olive oil. The loins of pork I'd butchered were crusted with fennel and served au jus—with a broth we whipped up with roasted pork bones done earlier in the day, a little white wine, some herbs, and aromatic vegetables. In the space of a few scary hot hours my fears had evaporated; I'd picked up a few new techniques and made a good friend. When the last table had been served, we cracked open a couple of cold beers as we cleaned up our stations. Joe was, like me, a proud Italian-American—a working-class guy from the boroughs. He had started out in butcher shops and catering halls in his native Queens. He wanted to learn more, so he enrolled in the Culinary Institute of America, and then worked in the city at a number of fine-dining restaurants where he learned French technique. Also like me, he found that the fancier places were not all they were cracked up to be. When the Nick & Toni's opportunity appeared, he jumped.

We wrapped up for the night and walked out together, chatting amiably, when I stopped dead in my tracks. A fancy blue sports coupe was parked in front of the restaurant. Oh shit!

Joe took one look at the expression on my face and made the world's quickest exit. He was a pro all right. He knew trouble when he saw it and knew when the right time to cut and run was, no questions asked. Unfortunately, I did not have that luxury.

Jenna stepped out of the car, unfolding all of her long legs as if in slow motion. She was, like most aspiring actresses, drawn to a good dramatic role. And what can possibly be more dramatic than the opportunity to play the scorned other woman? Turns out I was not a hard guy to track down. The late-model sports coupe was purchased with the proceeds from a national commercial she had landed before we met—and what's 125 miles of bumper-to-bumper traffic to be with a terrific catch like me. I should have put the kibosh on it right then and there, but she *had* made the drive, and I have an overdeveloped sense of guilt, and who says actors have a monopoly on being sucked into good theater? Plus she was looking extremely cute *goddammit*. Game on. I'd packed up my entire life and hauled it a hundred miles away from Manhattan just to get myself even deeper in a jam.

As the summer got rolling, Nick & Toni's became my culinary watershed. My first job was manning the wood-burning oven. This was more challenging than I had originally thought. To cook the food evenly, you had to keep it fired up perfectly with stacks of seasoned split wood. I'm no Boy Scout and I hadn't spent much time in any ski lodges. This kind of thing was new to me.

On one of the first really packed nights, I was trying to keep the fire at just the right temperature to get the food done fast and deliciously. To add to that confusion, I had to wear one of those Janet Jackson "Control" radio headsets to be in touch with the kitchen expediter. He was firing up order after order of roasted sea bass and herb chicken with pancetta and local bliss potatoes, barking the commands into my earpiece. Not to mention the appetizer specials. At one point I noticed I had six whole branzini that were barely browning and the orders were coming faster than I could even think about. The sweat was pouring down my head and I'm starting to freak because I look up and I can see the line stretching out the front door. Unfortunately, the only heat anywhere near that wood oven was my own internal body temperature, because the fire had dwindled to the point where you could barely roast a marshmallow on it. Ted stormed out of the kitchen and into the dining room to see what the backup was. He took one look at the dying fire and waved me back into the kitchen with his arm like a coach yanking a struggling rookie.

"Dude, no good," he said in his usual calm fashion. No histrionics. I'd failed at this task, but he simply moved me to another and went back to his work. Unlike some of the perfectionist, high-octane personalities I had met, Ted was a hands-on guy. He worked every station, and he was incredibly passionate about the food he served. Just watching him work and the relationship he had with food made me dig deeper into the job. I found myself coming in earlier and working later just to pick up new techniques and understand what made the simplicity of the Nick & Toni's menu such a strong draw.

Several weeks later the place is packed and I have earned my way back onto wood-oven duty. The dining room is so small that you have to be careful not to jab the six-foot-long oven spatula into someone's ear at the table beside it. I was serving some oven-roasted dishes when I see the movie director Steven Spielberg and his wife seated at one table. Even I have to pause, because I'm not sure I'd ever seen anyone that famous so close up. A moment later, I notice that Billy Joel and his wife are seated at another table! Billy Joel owns Long Island, and you can't grow up here and not have some feeling about him either way. His songs were on the radio every five minutes in the early '80s. It's sacrilege not to like Billy Joel, and even I had come around with his *52nd Street* album, which was essentially a jazz record.

So, at the end of the Joels' dinner, Billy and Christie make the requisite drive-by of the Spielbergs table for air kisses and the such, because East Hampton is a small town like any other where you say hi to your neighbors, except in East Hampton your neighbors arrive by Gulfstream jets and Porsche Turbo Carreras and Range Rovers. There is some rough terrain out there en route to wine tastings and fund-raisers. You need a vehicle that can take it. So the Joels and the Spielbergs kibitz for a few moments and say their farewells, and then Christie and Billy stroll out. As the door bangs shut, I hear someone nearby whisper, "I'm just *not* a fan!" Amazing. Everyone's a critic.

Everything about the place that I was happy to ignore, Gina reveled in. She'd be on the eight p.m. Saturday night express train from the city that had her at the restaurant by eleven p.m., a mere few hours after her last haircut. She'd take her seat at the bar, order up a Ketel One with olives, a fresh spinach salad, and settle right in. The staff loved her and she loved making the scene. Those Saturday nights were positively intoxicating, and sometimes we'd all end up at the beach in Amagansett, where the combination of warm salty ocean air, good champagne, and weed would keep us going until dawn.

The only problem was, the next morning Gina would push me out of bed way too early because we were losing precious rays. We'd meander over to Brent's in Amagansett for coffee and eggs and the paper. Then we'd order up sandwiches for a full-fledged day at the beach. If this sounds like a pretty perfect way to spend a summer, trust me, it was. But for one problem. Every single time I walked out of Brent's with Gina and our bag full of towels and lotion and hero sandwiches and the remains of the Sunday *Times*, I had to scan the parking lot to make sure a certain someone wasn't climbing out of a fancy blue coupe. Our ongoing drama may have been fine for her, but frankly, I was thinking one of these days the whole thing was going to blow up in my face. It had to be dealt with, soon. But as Gina and I settled into our lounge chairs and I pulled my shades over my sunburned nose, staring out at the waves crashing down on the beach, I thought, maybe tomorrow.

# Food and Marriage

My relationship with food up to this point had been one of purveyor-to-cook for the most part. The executive chef creates the menu, hands it off to the sous chef, who makes sure the cooks follow through. You take a look at the daily menu in the kitchen and call someone and say, "Give me three cases of this or twenty pounds of that," and the next morning it is delivered from Hunts Point Market in the Bronx or via an air freight company from Mexico or South America or God-knows-where in a refrigerated flat panel truck or a FedEx jet. Signed. Done.

Nick & Toni's introduced me to a whole new way of thinking as far as fresh food went. For starters, the backyard of the restaurant housed a garden that was abundant with freshly grown vegetables, tended lovingly by Farmer Jim, a passionate young guy who planted and raised and helped harvest the crop. So when you're doing a steak special with roasted peppers and you realize we're out of peppers, you merely walk out back and fill up a paper bag and get roasting. In our little garden alone, we grew Boston and Romaine lettuces; three varieties of summer squash; eggplants; beefsteak, cherry, and roma tomatoes; a dozen varieties of herbs: mint, buckets of basil, cilantro, chives, lavender, rosemary, thyme; and on and on. As a cook, it was cool to have this connection to the earth.

Of course, we could not be totally self-sufficient on a backyard garden, even one as meticulously cared for as ours, but that was the beauty of cooking on the East End. Eastern Long Island is blessed with a maritime microclimate, perfect for farming, and to the north by the Long Island Sound, winemaking. It's something in the soil or the ocean mists, or maybe it's the small size of the farms that allows for such excellence. Even the casual visitor to the Hamptons knows how good the local produce is. You'd see them lined up every weekend at roadside stands on Route 27 and at the Amagansett Market and the Springs for the sweet corn and tomatoes and strawberries bursting off the backs of wooden trailers all summer long. We had our local guys who kept us supplied daily with produce, and it was a joy for me to cook with such ingredients.

The same applied for the local seafood, some of the best around, as far I was concerned. My tenure at Margaux had provided me with an understanding of exotic seafood from around the world, and how to prepare it with elaborate concoctions of sauces thickened with cream and butter, and daylong reductions and delicate broths. Nick & Toni's showed me the beauty of simpler preparations made with whatever came in locally from Montauk, home of one of the oldest working fishing fleets in the country, located just a few miles down the road from us at the tip of Long Island. Today they bill it as "day boat" fish, as if someone just discovered the art of fishing, but out on the Island that's the only fish you get. Our guy would drive into town after his night's work on his *Boston Whaler* and unload his pickup truck heavy with coolers of striped bass and flounder and fluke and fat juicy scallops. We'd sauté in a little butter and olive oil and chop in fresh herbs from the garden, and there you go, we had the daily special—Sea Scallops with Herbs.

I tried to carry that sensibility over into all of my cooking. Diners and food critics alike were already jumping on the locavore bandwagon. If you can't grow it and serve it sustainably, not only were you depleting natural resources by overfishing and shipping unnaturally grown foods eight thousand miles by container ship, but you were also serving food that was not meant to be served locally. On Long Island, we had the means to do it right. If only my personal life were as sustainable as that.

Jenna and I had arrived at a place where we both knew it had to end, but we were failing miserably at bringing that about. She'd steal her way out when Gina was in the city, which was incredibly stressful for me. I was losing weight, and friends were starting to ask if anything was wrong. I blamed it on the frantic work schedule, keeping my dual existence under wraps. I actually longed for the chance to finish work at midnight on a Saturday and have two whole days off to chill out. As if Jenna would have any part of that. Not that I didn't encourage her. I worked with addicts of all kinds. Cooks who hit their day beers at six a.m., managers getting their sports bets in or slipping out every hour for a fat joint. I suppose cooking requires an addictive personality. My personal addiction was wrapped in the guise of a five-foot-nine actress with a fancy sports coupe and matching blue eyes.

One Saturday night when Gina had stayed in the city, I walked out of the restaurant at midnight, worn to shit and secretly hoping that maybe Jenna had gotten hung up and decided to bail. No such luck. She had hightailed it out after her shift ended and had been waiting for me for an hour, and she was pissed off. We drove in her car to a secluded spot of beach. I was pensive and guilty and not saying very much. I was over this whole thing and I certainly wasn't about to take her to the spot where my work friends congregated on Saturday nights after a long shift. Okay, maybe just one more fix. A crisp bottle of Veuve and a healthy romp on the beach did wonders for her mood and mine temporarily, but there were fifteen more hours of weekend to go. What were we supposed to do now?

We stopped by the restaurant to pick up my car. The night porter who was busy hosing down the kitchen floor mats outside the restaurant looked at me with this disapproving expression. Christ, even the help was sitting in judgment. I was starting to wonder what it would take to shake me out of this.

No doubt there'd be a half dozen out-of-town visitors camped out all over my place, so on a whim I pulled into a ramshackle motel I'd passed about a million times before. The place was a single-story shack trap with an unweeded, glass-strewn parking lot and a loud buzzing neon sign with the word "No" flickering on and off intermittently. I wondered if it was a biblical warning but pulled in to explore all the same.

"What the hell is this?" Jenna demanded.

"Well it's not the Plaza and there won't be cocktails on the terrace," I joked. I guess her sense of humor was starting to fade. Still, I got out of the car to explore. There turned out to be one room available. When the clerk asked me for my license plate number I started to write down the actual plate and then thought better of it. Now I was becoming truly paranoid. As if Tony Perkins behind the front desk was going to do a DMV search at three a.m. to announce to the world that the sous chef at Nick & Toni's was having an affair. I paid in cash anyway.

Jenna was furious as I led her into the musty room, and who could blame her. Even I was wondering what kind of bugs we might both end up with after we crawled between the sheets. Six more hours until daylight. I found myself half hoping that Gina would show up in the parking lot and we could put an end to the whole miserable charade. Why was I putting myself through this, jeopardizing my marriage and whatever was left of my self-respect? Was I just trying to make up for all those years when I felt life was passing me by? The go-nowhere jobs, the women I never had a chance at, the squandered educational opportunities? I was attempting to steal back a decade long ago gone.

The glorious summer of my discontent sped by like a riptide. It had become the perfect combination of professional dedication and complete psychological avoidance. My shrink would have had a field day, were she not off vacationing in Positano. Maybe we could compare recipes when she got back.

Labor Day weekend rolled around faster than I ever would have dreamed or hoped. My mom and dad finally made it out one weeknight right before the end of the season. They had never been to Nick & Toni's before, but now because of me they had some inkling of its reputation. My mom studied the menu like it was a traffic summons, listened to the five or six specials of the evening, and finally asked if they had any "fillet." I told the waiter she would have the striped bass. As I watched them enjoy their meal in the midst of all the celebrities and moguls and minimoguls, I realized just how proud I had made them. They had made me proud as well. I could sense, as they sat there enjoying their decaf espressos and crème brûlée with mint and fresh berries, that they got it. I happily escorted them to their car after dinner. I was so glad they came.

On the last weekend of the summer we were jammed to the gills. It had been a nonstop month of three hundred dinners a night, seven nights a week. The late-August Long Island air was drenched with humidity, the air-conditioning could barely contain it, and the kitchen was a sauna. The cooks were all crispy fried from stealing those last precious hours at the beach, and the August customers were the most demanding bunch of all. On the final Saturday night, we worked till we dropped. The wood-burning oven was running at 1,000 degrees from noon until midnight, and our local farmers were dropping off crates of summer corn and tomatoes and squash and zucchini blossoms. We were peeling and shucking and seeding and stuffing in every square inch of the kitchen, and the tables were turning over in droves. Celebrities large and small, famous and infamous, came by for one last taste. And then, just like that, it was done. As if someone had flipped a switch. Party over. I literally stood on the deck of the restaurant watching the receding line of expensive, European red taillights heading west, en route to Manhattan. Back at the end of that stream of lights, some hundred miles away at the Midtown Tunnel, I had a life on hold that was beckoning, and my excuses for avoiding it were dwindling. Clearly I was going to have to deal with this.

On the Tuesday night following Labor Day, Jeff Salaway threw the annual staff blowout. It was at the sprawling home of one of our best and most loyal customers. No celebrity A-list was invited. It was just for us. The wine and beer and tequila flowed. The tables were abundant with all the glorious foods of summer, all provided by a local caterer so that none of us had to lift a finger. It was a no-holds-barred affair, the end of summer camp—a jubilant celebration.

Gina decided not to haul out for the bash. She had found us a new apartment in the East Village and was already getting back into her city routine—summer put away, new styles waiting to be coiffed as the fall season filtered in. I was on my own. The backyard surrounding the pool was lit like a scene from *The Great Gatsby*, and the sounds of blaring salsa echoed across the estate. I stood alone and took it all in. I was drinking tequila, something I almost never did, but at that moment I had a ray of clarity as to why it was so popular with the staff.

My reverie was broken when I felt the meaty hands of Joe tighten around my waist. He was joined by several other line cooks, who picked me up like a side of beef. Against my laughing protestations they carried me to the pool and with the crowd roaring, at the count of three, launched me into the air. I landed with a splash and came up sputtering to the surface. I floated there on my back, fully dressed, above the shimmering green lights, the water cool and refreshing as it ran down my face. I stared up from the serene pool waters at my newfound summer family and wondered, what the fuck do I do now?

# The Conversation

The Waverly Inn and its unstoppable buzz hardly happened overnight. While the owners, myself included, certainly set out to create a successful restaurant, the last thing on our minds was a celebrity outpost beyond anyone's wildest dreams.

Did I ever imagine that I'd add the title of "owner" to my gradually expanding cooking résumé? At the outset I had never even considered it. It was my passion for food that drew me into the business when I chucked my corporate career in favor of more creative climes. Like any neophyte to the business, I was actually operating under the assumption that if you love a good meal, enjoy entertaining a few friends, and can learn some basic knife skills, the rest would follow. How naïve was I, along with every other person who ever thought opening a restaurant was a simple endeavor.

In fact, the only thing more challenging than opening a restaurant in the first place is opening a restaurant in New York, as I would soon learn in tackling the Waverly. With all the attendant complications associated with food, multiply your problems by a thousand. The City of New York is uniquely set up to ensure that starting a small business is the most futile, time-consuming, and frustrating thing you will ever do in your professional life. Armed with this information, I and my new Waverly partners rolled up our sleeves and got to work.

From the beginning I was thankful that I had signed on with two guys named Sean and Eric, who were as imaginative as they were successful. They came to the table with years of experience running such far-flung and wildly popular operations as Bar Marmont in West Hollywood and The Park in Chelsea. I was truly fortunate to have these guys on my side, with their knack for opening and succeeding in neighborhoods on the fringe. They knew how to get it done, and we were starting from scratch, literally. We had a decent lease on a quiet corner in highly desirable Greenwich Village. That was the good news. But the former restaurant occupying that corner—Ye Olde Waverly Inn—had died an ignominious death, fading from view as so many New York places do. What we had to start with was a dusty ground-floor space, a defunct kitchen, a courtyard with a towering hundred-foot oak tree poking through a shredded tarp acting as a ceiling, and room for maybe a hundred seats. No way could anyone look at this mess and think it would be easy. And it was not.

Sean and Eric tended to operate in lockstep, which probably explained all their previous successes. Sean was more the conceptual thinker and Eric was the roll-up-your-sleeves let's-do-it-now guy, but depending on the nature of each individual challenge, they could exchange roles easily. Challenge number one was pure logistics. Opening a restaurant requires a pocketful of readily accessible cash and patience beyond belief. You could spend three weeks waiting for an inspector to approve your exhaust hood, and on the day he finally comes, you wait ten hours and it turns out he showed up while you were taking a leak and he didn't even bother to knock. Would you like to reschedule? We have an opening in four months.

Eric and Sean had the connections from all of their other New York properties to overcome most of the bureaucratic red tape and paperwork.

Along with their vision, they brought three different lawyers—one to form the corporation, one for the liquor authority, and one to navigate the tangle of rules and regulations of the New York City Buildings Department. They also brought expediters, architects, designers, painters, air-conditioning specialists, guys to clean the grease traps—even an artist whose claim to fame was expertly hand-painting the No Smoking and Employees Must Wash Hands signs. We employed awning guys, wood polishers, craftsmen, electricians, welders, plate-glass specialists, a horticulturist, and a florist. But even as the plans and permits were coming together, none of us was sure exactly what The Waverly was going to be. Least of all me.

Sean had heard from the landlord that one of the people who had shown interest in the property before us was a neighbor, West Village fixture and publishing legend Graydon Carter. This information might not have meant a lot to the traditional restaurateur, but Sean was always floating a dozen interesting ideas in his head, and this connection had potential. He got on the horn to Graydon and the two had a meeting. A day later Sean walked into the place and announced we had a new partner. Arguably, that was the day the Waverly Inn was reborn.

Amid all the dust and construction wreckage that still comprised the interior of the place, a six p.m. meeting was called. Eric and I pushed the old tables and chairs into a sort of boardroom table. Graydon Carter arrived from wherever someone of Graydon Carter's stature arrives at the end of an insanely busy publishing workday. Sean was the last to show, and he brought a fifth member of the team, a dapper-looking gentleman wearing an off-white panama hat. His name was Emil and he wore a serious expression that complemented his unidentifiable European accent. He had apparently opened several of Sean and Eric's places a decade earlier. He also had experience as a general contractor, among other things. I looked on with cautious optimism at this disparate crew, hardly able to believe that somehow I was involved in this endeavor.

It was Sean who took the lead, marching us around the place, waving his arms dramatically where he envisioned a row of red leather banquettes. Emil watched as quietly as I did, letting the visionaries do their thing. We all marched out to the back patio where the tree, poking a hundred feet into the sky, righteously dominated the space, almost as if it were watching over us. Anyone who walks into that room can't help but fall in love with that tree. One can only imagine what it has seen since the first Waverly Inn was established in 1920.

We returned to our makeshift boardroom. Graydon gently set his expensive suit jacket down on a sawhorse and rolled up his shirtsleeves. He pulled out a cigarette and tapped it thoughtfully on the palm of his hand. I had never met him before, but I was a fan of *Spy* magazine, which he started in the late 1980s. Like its founder, it was smart, funny, and ironic. He definitely had my attention.

"Nuts in ceramic ramekins on the bar," he barked out finally, in his gruff, unmistakable voice. "Old-fashioned cocktails in elegant small glasses. Gin Rickys. Manhattans. Martinis ice cold. And no Long Island Ice Teas, for goodness sakes," he continued, growling. "We'll do a classic menu. And don't give me any of that chef'd-up nonsense. I want real food. We'll be a neighborhood place. Like Elaine's in the seventies." Graydon didn't know me, and he was not really a customer of Sean and Eric's other bustling, vigorous, noisy places. His taste leaned more toward the Four Seasons and La Grenouille for lunch. He favored 21, and, in London, Le Caprice and The Ivy. I had my work cut out for me.

Graydon got up and peered at a large, scarred wall above where Sean's imaginary red leather banquettes were going to be. "We'll soundproof the place to keep things at a reasonable level," he announced. "I'll get Ed Sorel to do a mural." He was referring to the famous artist whose work graced *Vanity Fair*, *The New Yorker*, and every other urbane fashionable magazine that had made New York the literary capital of the world. I was starting to sense his vision. We all were.

You could almost feel The Waverly buzz even in that dust-covered, hollowed-out construction area.

The meeting lasted less than an hour. I don't think Emil and I said two words. We simply watched, taking mental notes as the principals mapped out their plans. Sean took a call on his cell. Graydon and Eric rested their elbows on the bar and chatted about art and New York and some very influential people who had changed the curvature of the earth's surface but whom I'd never even heard of. Emil and I nodded at each other with guarded respect—recognition that someone was going to have to execute this grand vision, and that someone was going to be us.

# Park Babylon South

Driving westbound on the Long Island Expressway back to the city, my Nick & Toni's summer vacation was already fading. I had business on my mind. Finding a permanent job, for one. Repairing my marriage and putting an end to my affair for another. Gina had yet again exceeded expectations as far as managing our lives. She had found us a terrific duplex apartment in a funky cool East Village neighborhood near Avenue A. The place was spacious and old with great original tenement details, but updated and modern with an industrial spiral steel staircase leading to the large upstairs loft bedroom that looked out on a tree-lined street. It was a sweet home and I'd had a great summer and I desperately wished I was less-conflicted than I was as I unpacked my bags to move in.

Distancing myself from Jenna was going to be trickier than I had hoped, since she was the one who had introduced me to one of New York's hottest up-and-coming restaurateurs in the first place. Dan Benson owned two very busy restaurants on the Upper East Side, a seafood spot and another place that was known for its terrific rotisserie chicken. He was a semi-regular at Nick & Toni's, and I had met him when Jenna had taken me to his house to hang out poolside. He was a warm and personable guy, in great physical shape, completely self-assured, and you just knew he was going places—and if you didn't, he'd be happy to tell you all about it.

Jenna had been hired by Dan to establish the reservationist's duties at his soon-to-open new restaurant called Park South, a cavernous space located on lower Park Avenue. This area of the city was marked by grand old cast-iron buildings that housed banks, publishing companies, and advertising agencies. When I was back in town, Jenna informed me there might be a slot at his new place, so I contacted him and we met for breakfast. He knew my work from Nick & Toni's, so that wasn't an issue. Without a lot of fanfare I told him what I wanted to earn. He said fine, shook my hand, and as I was getting up to leave, still holding my hand he squeezed it a little tighter and said, "It will never be this easy to get money from me again." He flashed me his megawatt smile and it was a done deal.

I came on board as executive sous chef under Jimmy Baxis, who was recruited after Dan's first choice dropped out to open his own place. Jimmy was Paul Newman handsome with blue eyes—a thick-skinned half-Greek, half-Italian—whom Dan had wrested away from the three-star fish restaurant Voiage. As it turned out, Jimmy had just started there when he got Dan's offer, so it would be at least a month before he could pull up roots and begin at Park South full-time. That gave me time to either make a mark or crap out. So yet again I found myself thrown into construction mode as I opened my third restaurant in as many years.

The first thing I noticed about Dan was that he knew every detail about everything, including how to do most people's jobs better than they knew themselves. He was not afraid to roll up his sleeves and get dirty, which he did a lot. A complete madman and control freak with a manic obsession about every detail that was going into his place, he was very fond of the first person possessive, as in, "This is how we do things at 'MY Restaurant,' 'MY business,' 'MY bar.' " I'd arrive in the kitchen where a new dishwashing sink was being installed and Dan would be hovering over the plumber, screaming at him that they needed a three-quarter-inch fitted-pipe couplet to pass fire code. Never mind that he was telling this to a twenty-year veteran of the plumber's union. The scary thing was, Dan was right. He was always right. No detail was too small for him to ream someone out, throw a tantrum, or just heave a few pots for good measure.

As executive sous chef my job was to hire the staff and get the place up and running. To understand the task, you need to understand the size of the place. It was positively daunting, an enormous floor space—something like two hundred seats, which meant I had to bring in a staff larger than any I had ever worked with before.

Staffing a restaurant is like a Broadway cattle call. New York is home to more waiters, waitresses, hostesses, line cooks, dishwashers, and coat check girls than you could possibly imagine. The only problem was that they were all in rehearsal all the time. "What's your availability?" I'd ask, and yet another gorgeous young aspiring actress would say, "Well, let's see. I have class Mondays, Wednesdays, and Fridays, six to nine p.m. and readings Tuesday mornings from ten to two. Oh, and I can't work Sundays because I have tap dance. Will that be OK?"

"Great, why don't we just open the restaurant by appointment only," I'd reply.

Since the chef was still not on board full-time, my other gargantuan task was hiring the kitchen staff. Dan Benson did not know the meaning of thinking small. He was planning to do lunch and dinner and a late-night bar menu *and* weekend brunches. I was in the market for at least twenty cooks. You'd think the owner of such an ambitious operation would defer to his executive sous chef for hiring this far down the line. Not a chance. I liked a guy for the relatively low job of pantry cook. This requires mainly making salads and toasting up croutons. Not exactly brain surgery. Dan sees me talking to the candidate and pulls me over and says, "See the shoes on that guy, Johnny? Think about whether you really want him in the kitchen." So I look at the guy's shoes. They're beat-up wingtips that he probably got from a consignment shop on the Lower East Side. He looks bohemian to me, hardly a stretch in this business. Somehow it did not seem relevant to his ability to wash and dry salad greens. So when Mr. Wingtip crapped out a month later, I had Dan Benson barking in my ear saying, "You see, you see, I told you!"

He reviewed every hire, every cook, every busboy, and especially every coat check girl. He even vetted Raj, our little Punjabi coffee guy who screwed up one night and served ten lukewarm cappuccinos to a table of Dan's friends. BIG mistake. It was brutal watching Raj endure Dan's wrath, but then again, cold cappuccino is never an option.

Our butcher, Diego, was also one of my hires. He came to me with experience at several excellent and well-thought-of places, and his résumé did not have a lot of skipping around. He couldn't have been more pleasant. On the day I hired him Dan walks by and sees me interviewing. He pulls me over and says, "Johnny, he's a drunk. Forget it." I'd just about had it up to my ass with this insane micromanaging and I said, "Dan, please, honestly, just let me do my job?" Dan was very respectful to me and he cut me slack on this one. Diego worked for three solid months and didn't miss a day. Then, out of the blue, one Friday afternoon—payday—he picks up his check, asks to go cash it just as he had every other week for three months, and disappeared. For good! I tried to cover it up out of pure embarrassment, but there I was doing Diego's job at a quarter the speed and one-tenth the efficiency when right on schedule Dan comes around the corner giving me "the look." Exasperated I said, "Please don't say it."

Park South finally opened and the Benson-driven throngs poured in en masse. Dan may have been manic and controlling and obsessive, but he knew how to start and run a restaurant. Foodwise, we were basically a chicken-and-pizza emporium: poached chicken in the salad, grilled chicken on the pizza, sautéed chicken on top of the pasta. Pan-roasted chicken, Cobb salad with chicken, chicken on focaccia. But it was good chicken and pretty legit pizza, and all at prices that glitzy young people could afford, which made the place even more of a draw. The bar was packed with New York's beautiful and young and upwardly mobile lookers, and we were staffed up with an equally appealing entourage of wait- and bar staff. The array of temptations was unbelievably stunning and plentiful, and that was not including the occasional tryst with Jenna, who still had me pegged as her provider du jour.

Sadly, this all pointed to the fact that after several years of ardent marital vacillation, and an affair that was now more than half a year in, I had no business being married any longer. For all I knew, Gina had figured this out and perhaps had even been conducting her own illicit affairs to boot. This, however, was merely projection and rationalization of my own shit behavior. The deathly silence that had become our marriage led us into a brief bout of counseling, but it was no shock or surprise when after a few months we decided to separate. I'd like to say that this threw me into a life crisis that forced me to mature and reconcile, and that led us to a wiser, better place. The truth was slightly different.

Gina decided that I should keep the East 9th Street apartment while she found a new place to live. This provided an easy place for me and Jenna to still occasionally steal away for an hour's indulgence, which turned out to be another phenomenally bad idea on my part. Gina, who still had her keys, walked in on us one lazy afternoon when she was stopping by to pick up some dry cleaning she had left. She took one look, sized up the situation, and went on a rampage, beating at me with her fists in a rage—and then she went after Jenna, who had locked herself in the bathroom, cowering. Finally, Gina left. Jenna left. And I stood there in silence for about ten minutes contemplating the emotional carnage. Then I took a shower and went to work, amazed that I could even do that.

I spent the next few weeks in a listless, melancholic malaise. Jenna and I put a halt to our affair, cold turkey. I was served papers from Gina in front of the bar at Park South. How appropriate. We were divorced a year later without so much as a sentence uttered between us. My wife, a person I had known since high school, dated for five years and been married to for more than four years, was gone. The operatic melodrama had ended, leaving me more than a little traumatized. So began my period of uncontested craziness, latent adolescence, and devolving morality.

I decided to keep the apartment and, in no particular order, took up partying, womanizing, and drinking. While it provided delightfully entertaining fodder for my shrink, it was not exactly a boon to my health. Park South was on fire. We were doing hundreds upon hundreds of dinners a night and the place was so popular that it literally changed the landscape of lower Park Avenue. Other, copycat places started to move in and drive up the rents. We had become bar and canteen to all the modeling agencies that existed in that stretch of Manhattan and this just added to the allure and craziness.

One night Jimmy, the chef, and I were trying to figure out how the hell we could get the food out faster from the kitchen, partly to please the clientele, but mostly to keep Dan off our asses. We had a very popular tuna dish (the chicken of the sea) that required a pan sauce of shallots, white wine, and butter that had to be made individually for every single order. It was absolutely gumming up the works, so we decided to simplify the process. We'd make the butter sauce in advance, as most restaurants do. You reduce the wine and shallots, whisk in the butter, and put it all in a bain-marie—a double boiler that we used to keep it warm until it's time to sauce the dish—and boom, tuna out. We decided not to tell Dan because we knew he wouldn't like it, and besides, we were positive he wouldn't know the difference anyway. Thirty-seven tuna dishes later he comes into the kitchen on the warpath.

"What the fuck are you guys doing?" he screamed. "You're ruining MY business. You fucked up MY tuna!"

How did he know? Dan had his finger on the pulse of every last thing that went on in his empire. Every night he would ask twenty-five or thirty customers, "What do you think of this, what do you think of that?" He asked every last person their opinion and he listened and remembered it all. Obviously one customer had offered a negative review of the tuna. So ended our brilliant concept of ever making a sauce in advance.

Even with our enormous staff, every day and night I was falling further and further behind. I was working six and sometimes seven days a week, lunch and dinner and Sunday brunch, the bane of the sous chef's existence. Eggs forty-seven ways, French toast, omelets, and the entire rest of the menu. It was an absolute nightmare. We had a dozen cooks per shift churning it out to fifteen waitresses in short black skirts and sexy starched white blouses who dumped it on the table and followed it up with coffee service from two state-of-the-art espresso machines: latte this and decaf that, whipped cream, low-fat, nonfat, double mochaccinos, and cafés au lait, all topped off with desserts flying out as fast as we could serve them. The busboys crumbed those tables clean and the wait was an hour or more. As much as I was dying out there, through all of it I was learning about the restaurant as commerce.

Like everything else, Dan was maniacal about food costs, and you couldn't plate an extra carrot without him noticing. He'd drill it into our heads exactly what that meant. There would be reports every week, and God help us if you were off one percentage point. There would be a meeting, a phone call, or at the very least an e-mail explaining in the most colorful and vicious language where the margin should be. At this level of business, one percent was about a million bucks a year in lost revenue. In the midst of a lunch crush, Dan would walk into the kitchen in his shirtsleeves and tie and observe the activity. Then he'd say to me, "Johnny, how many guys you got working on the line?" And I'd look over through the chaos and say, "Three." And he'd pause for about one microsecond and say, "Okay, next week it's two." I always assumed he'd done the math in his head and we'd just saved another half-mil. A great place to own, but this was becoming a brutal place to work.

I respected Dan. He rolled up his sleeves like anyone else and wasn't a know-it-all. He just happened to know it all. You have to be that way to run a profitable place and he was cleaning up. New Yorkers back then were making money hand over fist, and even those who weren't were spending like they were. Jenna and I were done, and I was drinking more than I ever had in my life while the restaurant was providing me a steady stream of friends and attractive young women who wanted to party often, and often all night long. Something was bound to give.

One night, not long after God-knows-who had left my apartment, I woke up at four a.m. in excruciating pain. I was alone and I had no idea what was wrong. Too embarrassed to call an ambulance, I crawled out the front door and found a taxi that took me to the emergency room down the street from my apartment. The ER doctor did a quick examination and announced that I was suffering from kidney stones. They pumped me full of morphine and abandoned me. I've never felt pain like that in my entire life. I realized no one even knew I was there. I called Jimmy, but I was in so much pain I could barely get the words out. I managed somehow to communicate the notion that I was in the hospital and I felt like I'd been impaled with a heavy blunt object near my right lower back, and he asked, "Does that mean you're not gonna be at work tonight?"

Later that day my hospital-appointed urologist, clad in all-black Armani, with an unidentifiable accent and an extraordinary amount of glossy hair gel, comes into my room and announces the stone is too big to pass. He is going to have to operate. Within the hour, two interns are prepping me for an epidural, but as they are about to insert the six-inch needle into my spine, Dr. Armani enters the OR in his scrubs and starts screaming at the anesthesiologist that he ordered general anesthesia, not a spinal. He's using words like "assholes" and "dickheads," and I'm all doped up, so it sounds suspiciously like I'm back in the kitchen, not an operating room. I don't even know if this is real or a nightmare.

I wake up six hours later, stoned out of my gourd on morphine, with a hole in my back, a tube going through it attached to a bag containing my own piss. My Catholic upbringing convinces me that this is some form of penance for my behavior, and I actually believed I deserved it. The doctor comes in to check on me, sporting yet another black ensemble, and I finally decide this guy is an asshole, not a sentiment one normally likes to associate with one's healthcare provider. I ask him how long for this bag and he tells me a month or so, and saunters out giving the youngish, cute-ish, red-haired nurse the once-over. I'm lying there staring at the institutional hospital blue walls and the lead paint peeling off the ceiling, and I'm thinking I've never missed a day of work in my life, and now look at me, pissing in a bag through a tube coming out of my back for a month. I closed my eyes and reached for the morphine drip.

# French Roast

In time, I recovered from my kidney stones, but Park South needed a different kind of fix. There were too many sixteen-hour workdays, too many brunches, lunches, and dinners. Too much booze, too many all-nighters, too many easy opportunities with women I had no business being with. Too much of Dan Benson's craziness and micromanaging. I was getting burned out on the scene, and the work was no longer stimulating. With Jimmy at the helm, there was no chance I was moving up anytime soon. It had been four years since I'd completed my New School cooking class and I wasn't even sure I wanted to continue. Then I met François.

He represented a new wave of international pan-European style that was infiltrating New York. He had already opened a couple of Euro-influenced eateries that featured a bistro menu, Ibiza-style house music complete with subwoofers, and a crowd well known to many as Eurotrash. One of his popular spots, Le Petite Ami, anchored a bustling corner downtown and had become a staple of the trendy SoHo diet. The only problem was that its clientele, mostly models, were constantly *on* a diet—consisting mainly of champagne, martinis, and cocaine. The models came for the scene and they were trailed by swarthy English-as-a-second language guys with snug, buttery leather motorcycle jackets and fitted white cotton shirts unbuttoned to their waists. Everyone was having a great time, but the lack of food sales from the French-Moroccan–infused menu was proving to be a deterrent to anything that resembled profitability. François liked the food at Park South, but he could not afford a chef the likes of Jimmy Baxis, so he approached me to revamp Ami's weary menu.

He came with a management team: two six-foot-tall, striking Scandinavian women serving as "partners" in his new venture. It wasn't clear to me whether their contribution was going to be financial or sartorial, but clearly the three of them were in cahoots. I took my one and only day off from work and invited the triumvirate to my East Village apartment to sample a tasting menu that I had frantically improvised. My kitchen was about as large as a galley in a small sailboat, but my ambitions were large, and I went all out. The centerpiece was a whole roasted red snapper for two. I've always liked dishes for two, because you can serve two guests as fast as one and people love to share. To do a whole fish you need scorching high heat to really crisp the skin and get that tasty caramelization. I blasted my home oven as high as I could, but I guess it hadn't been cleaned in a while, and the apartment filled with so much oily billowing smoke that the smoke alarms were going off on two floors. You could barely see the food I served to my potential future bosses lined up in a row on my cheesy, new bachelor-pad black leather couch. We had to open all the windows and the door, and we were coughing and laughing so hard that we could barely eat. I was hired on the spot.

This was no small deal, my first shot as chef at a major New York restaurant. François shut down Ami for some minor remodeling. While he and the Scandinavians focused on the look of the forty-five-seat duplex space, I took my shot at creating my first menu. I'd been hired for the feel of the food at Park South, so in that sense the die was cast.

François was typically Parisian down to his afternoon Pernod and a trail of stubbed-out Gauloises, but he was ready to embrace a more American-style restaurant. This didn't necessarily mean I could reinvent the wheel, but rather bring my own touch to his place by interpreting dishes that people tend to enjoy and are familiar with, dishes we can get out of the kitchen in a timely way. I tinkered with a grilled pizza that I'd had at the famous Il Forno in Providence, Rhode Island. I loved the idea of raw dough on a hot grill and I devised a number of innovative toppings to add some panache. I did a hangar steak marinated in a Barolo wine, a take on the barbecues my family used to prepare when I was a kid. We had a roasted half chicken with pancetta, sea salt, and fruity olive oil, pan-roasted until it was crispy as a potato chip on the outside and dripping with juices when you bit into it. This was stolen directly from Nick & Toni's. It was simply that good. It works amazingly well with roasted red bliss potatoes and rosemary, the flavors melding perfectly. Enjoying my newfound autonomy, I insisted that François purchase a new convection oven for the miniscule kitchen at Le Petite Ami. He conceded and we took a little field trip to the Bowery in lower Manhattan where all the restaurant supply houses were. We found what we needed and he paid cash on the spot. This was becoming fun. I would now be able to cook faster and hotter and play with and perfect some new food.

For the ultracritical job of sous chef I poached my good friend Ari from Park South. He had gotten me through many a busy night working multiple stations without complaint. Lately he'd been having all sorts of run-ins with Jimmy, so basically I was doing both of them a favor and taking them out of their respective miseries. Ari was a passionate, decent cook, with a good work ethic. I felt I could count on him, despite the fact that he smoked about an ounce of weed a day before work. One month after Ari started, one Friday night he didn't show up. That turned into Saturday night. When he finally waltzed in Sunday, his eyes as red as a sustainably grown organic beet, I went nearly ballistic. "Where the fuck have you been?" I asked.

"Dude, Jerry died," he said morosely, as if I knew. Jerry? Did we have a mutual acquaintance named Jerry? I went off on him. "Jerry the butcher? Jerry the guy that delivers the meat? Jerry my long-lost uncle? Who the fuck is Jerry?" It turned out that Jerry was Jerry Garcia, the lead guitarist of the Grateful Dead and spiritual leader of all things cannabis. Ari had been sitting vigil in Central Park getting baked with every other Deadhead in New York all weekend long. Silly me, I should have known. "Just get dressed" was all I could say. Maybe Dan Benson was right. I should have checked those shoes.

From Margaux I brought in Gavin, who was between jobs and really knew how to cook. I hired a new kid named Tom for the pantry, to make the salads and appetizers and desserts. He had walked in off the street from a local cooking school and reminded me a lot of my early days on the job at Yellowfingers. I remembered Rezbi's disdain for these guys. On the other hand, I needed cooks. Cooking school suddenly seemed the place to look, though, as predicted, it came at a price.

We were doing a Thai-influenced spicy calamari appetizer that I had picked up from two Thai brother cooks at Park South. It was the simplest of preparations, just some deep-fried spicy calamari with a soy-and-fish-sauce-based dressing, garnished with a fresh lime wedge. We were testing it one busy night and Cooking School Tom announces to me, as if he were just made Speaker of the House, "Chef, eighty-six the calamari." Annoyed to no end I asked him why, since I had just that morning ordered and cleaned ten pounds of calamari myself. You don't want to order too little because you'll run out and you don't want to order too much because it will go bad. I knew I had ordered the right amount. Tom replied, "Uhhh, because we're out of lime wedges?"

I looked at him, trying to remain calm, and said, "You're going to let ten pounds of perfectly fresh squid rot in the walk-in box because you don't have a lime wedge to put on the plate?" The problem with cooking school is that they don't train you to run out to the nearest corner store and buy out their inventory of whatever product you need, or steal it if they won't sell it to you. I did my best to be merciful to the rookie that I once was as I sent him down the street for limes.

François and the Scandinavian-style team took care of hiring the most beautiful bartenders and waitstaff New York had to offer, and we reopened on a warm spring night. The food was good and the buzz was good, but what I had not counted on was what is sometimes known in New York as "French service." This simply translates into no service or, in the best-case scenario, rude, slow service. I had just come out of the manic obsessive headspace of Dan Benson, who measured waiter-service time with a stopwatch calibrated to tenths of a second and calculated the waitstaff cost-to-meal ratio every fifteen minutes. Service at the rekindled Le Petite Ami was spotty at best and nonexistent and surly on the average. Not that you could blame the staff. They needed to smoke and lounge about and get chatted up by the waif-and-stubble crowd, so really it was a win-win for them.

Take for example, Martin, or rather, Mar-teen—a tall, wavy-haired Provençal waiter who probably never would have landed a job but for his French connection with François. He preferred to wear his own clothes over the required uniform and naturally no one protested. He favored dark fitted shirts and patterned neckerchiefs, and every now and then someone would have to literally peel him off some gorgeous thing so he could take the food order from the next table. I had little say in these front-of-the-house dilemmas and we were lucky to get through one seating a night, but the odd thing was, no one seemed to care. My food would often be sitting in the service pass under the infrared heat lamps to keep it warm, plated and ready to go without so much as a waiter in sight. If there was one thing that I had learned to do well and efficiently above all else, it was to move units. How many times have you sat in a restaurant with someone, maybe your distant relatives or a business associate armed with vacation photos—and you just wanted to eat and get the hell out of there, and you wait and wait and wait.

At Ami I was still operating under the assumption that someone actually cared about our food. Finally one night I was so frustrated that I ran roughshod over a poor runner named Tariq. Tables would get up and leave, he took so long to bus his station. I read him the riot act and explained that if tables don't get cleared, we can't serve the guests their dinner entrées, which are stuck under the heat lamps growing old. And if we don't turn over more tables, then we don't make more money and then we go out of business and no one has a job anymore. I think Tariq got that last bit. I looked out of the kitchen an hour later and saw him wrestling a plate still full of a half-eaten grilled pizza away from a well-dressed fashion-editorial type. I tore out several tufts of my own hair as I returned to the backed-up boiler room of a kitchen.

The Ami gig started out fine, and I certainly learned a fair amount in my first real assignment as chef. But pretty soon the place spun out of control and reverted back to exactly what François had tried to change in the first place. We were jammed to the gills with the guys in motorcycle jackets and ponytails buying drinks for the girls in miniskirts and ponytails, and they were all smoking and shouting and having sex in the bathrooms. No one cared a rat's ass about the food, and that mood infiltrated the kitchen really fast. Pretty soon it felt more like I was going to a party instead of a job and, frankly, why fight it? Everyone was having such a good time. Of course it couldn't last.

I knew last call was inevitable when we started getting regular visits from Herbie, the very nervous, very German silent partner, bookkeeper, and voice of reason. "Zee hangar steak and zee too-na, ees gut to go," he'd tell me. It was becoming clear that we'd all "gut to go" soon.

One night right after the kitchen had closed, I was hanging out with the bulk of my cook staff, sitting at the upstairs bar drinking whatever few profits were left. I'd been waiting ten minutes for a refill on my vodka tonic with lime because the bartender, Diane, had disappeared into the bathroom with one of the motorcycle jacket guys. Service did not seem to be forthcoming any time soon. A delicious brunette with blue eyes sat down next to me. I vaguely recognized her as one of the downtown neighborhood's local denizens. She had low-cut jeans and a high-cut shirt that exposed a bronzed and extraordinarily flat belly, and she seemed to recognize me. She said in a singsong voice that she *looved* the food here and happened to know that I was the chef. Then she asked me if it was true that chefs use all of their senses when they make love.

Honestly, you hear some pretty funny stuff when you put on that white jacket. I rolled my eyes and said, for me, about three out of five was the current norm, but I was working on it. Next thing I know we are canoodling on the banquette. I notice that the music is pounding and the bar is going great guns and we are disappearing in a cloud of smoke from all those imported cigarettes. Seniority has its benefits and I happened to have the key to the rooftop hatch. We got off the banquette and snuck around the bar to the kitchen entrance. We climbed the fire escape ladder and surfaced on the rooftop. It was a glorious summer's night and the Twin Towers and all of lower Manhattan were sparkling like a million little diamonds. Suffice it to say we had one of those mind-blowing New York City rooftop experiences that gives living here such appeal. A week or so later, less than a year after we opened, Ami shut its doors for good.

# Odd Pairing

The sparkle from the Ami high went flat faster than day-old champagne. Depressed, out of work, and with no place to go every night, it seemed like a good time to take stock. I started by reducing inventory, since my paychecks had dried up. I gave up the 9th Street apartment—ground zero of my wrecked marriage and a whole lot of questionable times beyond that. Gina was out of my life for good. Jenna was out of my life for good. And I found myself reflecting on what a messy and unnecessary end to my marriage I had brought about. My behavior was inexcusable, rash, and irresponsible. A good bout of unemployment gives you time to think about all sorts of things. I was ratcheting up the guilt big-time, and frankly, I deserved what I got and Gina deserved a lot better.

I took up residence in a tiny studio in a nondescript building on East 22nd Street that I sublet from Diana, the bartender at Ami. Like everyone else from that particular misadventure, she had to find work, and she'd taken off for L.A. to pursue her acting. She blew out of town so fast that I inherited all of her Pottery Barn furniture, including an enormous orange puffy couch with a white floral pattern that became the center of my late-night existence, sprawled out until all hours, remote in hand. All of a sudden I was dateless in the city. No "glitzy" chef job, as my friends would refer to it. The canteen was closed, and I thought about how much my social life was dependent on my vocation. I no longer had friends with nine-to-fives. I had left them all behind, or had they left me? I was now among the other single, starving, out-of-work artists, writers, actors, and cooks on the street. Broke, unshaven, newspaper tucked under my arm at noon, I went looking for a decent cup of coffee, wondering how long I could afford four-dollar macchiattos before the well ran dry. I would have to find a cheaper gym to not use. It was my first extended period of unemployment since working a day job. Regardless of whether your expertise was placing insurance executives or larding cod, it still landed you in the same dismal, pale blue Chelsea unemployment office collecting your paltry government check every other week.

One morning, at a coffee bar, I ran into Eve, a coworker from my days in East Hampton. She had heard of another restaurant opportunity. Jerry, a purported partner in one of New York's prestigious riverfront venues, had taken over a place in Bridgehampton, right on the main drag. The previous restaurants that occupied that space were the kind of Hamptons summer spots that changed hands every season, never establishing a reputation and never lasting beyond Labor Day. Hopefully Jerry had grander intentions.

I shaved and took the bus crosstown to the East River since cab fare was scarce for me at this point. I met with Jerry at "his" venerable establishment, although certain people who knew him would tell me he barely owned the brass on the toilet latches. Still, we had a delicious lunch and he offered me the chef's job for his new Bridgehampton spot, based on Eve's recommendation, my "mature" demeanor, and my emerging reputation as a very hardworking guy. The salary was a substantial step down. On the other hand, being able to afford lunch again would be a step up. I haggled with him to throw in a car allowance, since

I had long been without wheels and would need transportation to get around out at the beach. He acquiesced.

Arguably, leaving the city was the last thing that I wanted and yet exactly what I needed. Not only was I weary of the unemployment scene, but I was fearful of losing my cooking chops. You hear from many chefs that you are only as good as your last meal, and my last meal at Ami was not exactly Per Se. It's too bad you are not as good as your last drink. You can fall awfully fast in the restaurant business, wake up in no time flat and find yourself doing Sunday brunch at some food factory. Signing on with Jerry and his dubious reputation was a crapshoot, but frankly, there wasn't a line of restaurant owners breaking down the door to hire me. And I knew he wouldn't break my balls about the food. I felt the spring returning to my step even as I walked the entire way across town, back to my studio flat. In the space of a week I gave up the 22nd Street apartment, leased a new Beamer with a five-speed stick, and was back in business.

Several nights before I was to head out to Bridgehampton, Caroline, my buddy from Park South, invited me to a party down in Chinatown. I hadn't been into that scene for a long time, probably because my job had been such a party. But I hadn't seen her in a while and this seemed as good a chance as any to catch up. We buzzed our way into a nondescript, old, dilapidated building in Chinatown and were greeted by about a hundred crooked stairs rising like a ladder to the top floor. Out of breath, we summited in the midst of a booming downtown affair.

The place was a renovated factory with wide plank scraped-up floors painted a battleship gray. You could imagine some four-thousand-pound sewing machine or Letraset press sitting right there about a hundred years ago. The loft was shared by five waiter/artist/musician types, each of whom had set up a little camp in one part of the huge space. We fought our way to the makeshift bar for a drink. Caroline got ensconced in a conversation with some dude with a cleft in his chin about his upcoming audition, while I stood by, quietly nodding my head at all the right breaks in the conversation, pretending to be interested. But my attention in fact was drawn away to a woman standing alone by the bar. She was a towering, natural beauty who must have been at least five-foot-nine, not including her heels. She had this corn-fed look about her, very 1970s with her hair up, which gave her an *I Dream of Jeannie* vibe. What made her all the more standout was that she was wearing a silver lamé bra barely concealed by a high-cropped cotton halter top and faded blue hip-hugger bell-bottoms. She seemed supremely confident to be dressed like that, given it was a freezing cold night and everyone else was in black wool turtlenecks. Her face was so fresh and all-American she could have walked out of a Chevy pickup truck ad, having just split a cord of wood.

Caroline paused long enough in her conversation to notice me staring. "Johnny, you lose your nerve? Get over there," she said.

"What are you, nuts?" I replied. "Look at her. Who needs that?" My humiliation cup had runneth over, no doubt influenced by my weekly unemployment office visits. Still, that hair, that body. I figured I was one ridiculous opening line away from the number 6 train uptown and a good night's sleep. I ignored her for a little while and forgot about the whole thing until awhile later we found ourselves back to back sharing a little stool, drinks in hand.

Her name was Amy and in fact her corn-fed beauty was not some product of a midtown advertising agency. She really was from a small town in Nebraska and had found her way to New York after some swimsuit modeling jobs in L.A. She told me she loved Dr Pepper in the morning, which you just don't hear every day in New York, and which I found incredibly endearing. We talked, and we talked some more. She was young, too young, and yet I couldn't bring myself to ask her age. She laughed at all my jokes and was completely unimpressed with my career (we had a lot in common) and she was as uncomplicated as a

Kansas cornfield. I felt the first rumblings of a different kind of hunger brewing, like an oncoming summer thunderstorm. It was a welcome feeling that I hadn't experienced in a while.

It turned out she lived just a few blocks from me, and I offered to walk her home. When we got to her door on the top floor of a walkup, I asked her for her phone number. She obliged and politely, surprisingly, asked for mine. I wrote it down and then stood on tippy-toe and craned my neck to kiss her good night. As I walked out the door into the cold night I figured that was the last I would ever see of her. I didn't sweat it too much because she probably got about forty messages a night from guys like me. I could just picture my phone number on a scrap of paper buried in a drawer stuffed full of old Chinese food menus along with the pathetic attempts of half the male populace of New York scribbled on cocktail napkins. The odds didn't seem good.

A few days later I was with my friend Charlie and I told him I had met this young beauty who tended bar downtown. Charlie had a great sense of adventure and a genuine thirst for the opposite sex and could see no reason why we shouldn't be exploring this new avenue further. We found our way to a rough-and-tumble bar way downtown on the Lower East Side. We walked in the decayed storefront to some very loud vintage hip-hop playing over a formidable sound system. The place was dark and shadowy but even so I picked her out in a heartbeat, entertaining a packed bar full of young tattooed men and women. She was dressed in a pair of tight Levi's and a red, white, and blue stars-and-stripes bikini top. She was making a big show of pouring shots of Jack Daniel's and I wondered if I was a little out of my element.

Her place of work was a raucous, very racially integrated watering hole. The clientele struck me as a mix of drug dealers, junkies, and all of their friends and clients, which included a smattering of bankers and Wall Street types. I couldn't imagine I was going to pass muster with this mix and was ready to cut our losses and make a beeline to the door when she spotted me and waved us over. I was almost as surprised that she remembered me as I was that the brawny guy at the bar with a leering eye on her didn't beat me to a pulp on arrival. I guess there was something about her all-American looks that calmed the savage beast, because despite the sinister crowd, she seemed completely in control. There was a sweetness to her that transported me, even as she was swirling the Jack Daniel's bottle around like a six-shooter from a holster while occasionally flashing me smiles as if to say, "Hey, this is my day job, nothing more." At least in my smitten mind I wanted to believe that.

Charlie and I hung around until the place became so packed that we couldn't even hear ourselves talk. I figured since we hadn't been knifed, robbed, or worse we were ahead of the game. I leaned in between two menacing guys eyeballing Amy at the bar and I shouted over Public Enemy's "Fuck the Police" blaring out of the speakers, "Dinner tomorrow night?" Amazingly enough, she motioned with her head, lip-synching "Sure!"

It was the first time I had asked a woman out on a formal date in longer than I could remember—and never to the musical styling of Public Enemy. I found myself getting dressed nervously, wondering which pair of jeans made me look best. I dusted off my Frye boots because they had the kind of heel that would help a six-foot-minus guy like me kiss a six-foot-plus woman like her, should the situation present itself.

When I picked her up, she looked amazing in her jeans and thick turtleneck sweater, which somehow managed to reveal her former swimsuit model attributes all the same. She wore boots that negated whatever edge my Fryes might have given me. I took her to a sweet, romantic, inexpensive little French spot at 1st Avenue and 1st Street. It was everything you hope for and hate on a first date. She was sexy and adorable and interested, and she could eat. On the other hand, I was too nervous to get much down. I was knocking things over and spilling shit, and I pretty much felt like a kid on a prom date. It was fantastic!

I walked her home and she invited me in. Her roommate was an artist and the place was a complete shambles. It was small and dirty and smoke-filled with an ashtray the size of a Frisbee overflowing with half-smoked butts with lipstick stains on the tips of the filters. Beer bottles and paint tubes and half-finished masterpieces were draped all over the place. I didn't know if I should sit down or offer her my cleaning lady's phone number. I stayed until her roommate offered me something that sounded like drugs but I wasn't sure, and I decided to leave good enough alone.

A few days later I called again and invited her to my place. I made some simple tapas: a little tahini, eggplant, hummus, grilled sardines, and some crunchy fresh flatbread to sop up all the juice. We polished off a bottle of wine and then another and then she grabbed my hand, pulled me away from the table, and led me to my inherited orange puffy couch. The next morning . . . she was gone. I figured she was too hot and too sweet to be real and I would never see her again. Besides, I was starting my new gig and in the process of moving to the Hamptons anyway. So, being the cynic that I was, I didn't call.

A week later she tracked me down and told me she was really hurt. What the hell kind of girl did I think she was, anyway—someone who just jumped into the sack on a second date with every guy she met? I took the cue and invited her out to East Hampton, where I had just rented a two-bedroom house with a driveway made of rocks and a cedar deck. She came for the weekend and never left.

# Under New Management

Oceans sat at the corner of a busy intersection on the main thorough-fare to eastern Long Island, Route 27, at the end of a handful of shops that made up the entire village of Bridgehampton. It was easy to see why the place changed hands every summer. The interior was pleasant enough, but about as striking as a loaf of white bread. It was a perfectly average, rectangular room that took on whatever flavor the latest own-ers chose. There was a long bar at one end, maybe a hundred seats total, and a serviceable, if unspectacular kitchen.

Jerry, the principal owner, had convinced about fifty wealthy guys to fork over like fifty bucks each to get their hand in the restaurant busi-ness. I wasn't sure if this was good or bad, having so many bosses to please, but I had such a devil-may-care attitude at this point that there wasn't much to lose. Amy and I had become inseparable, and unlike the last time I had called the Hamptons home, there was not the distraction of often wishing I'd get hit by a truck. While we were playing house, I recruited a new friend of mine from the city, Jon Lopresti, to take the helm as sous chef. We had met through a mutual cook buddy and were both career changers who had done recruiting in our first careers. It was love and raging cynicism at first sight.

Whenever you are hired as chef, the owners give you some parameters of the kind of menu they envision. If they are not restaurant savvy, and sometimes even if they are, their suggestions will be basically what they and their friends like to eat nightly. When you have twenty-five owners or more, it can get pretty ridiculous. We'd have these sit-down meetings in the restaurant and whichever partners happened to be out at the beach that week would show up and one would say, "Hey, Johnny, how about sushi? I love sushi." Or another would say he had some great roasted wild game dish while he was on safari in Kenya. One of the partners' girlfriends was vegan, and while everyone was politely nodding their heads that we *must* take into consideration the vegetarian and vegan clientele, I'm thinking sure, with whose profits, as the fifty-pound bags of organic amaranth rot on the shelf because who else on earth is going to eat that stuff? They weren't a bad lot of guys actually, but their inexperience was obvious and a lot of their ideas had no relation whatsoever to what works in a professional kitchen. That was fine by me. We were going to make this place fly.

I called on all of my past years' influences to devise the menu. We did the crispy pan-roast chicken, giving the bird that extra something by preparing it with the bone in. You take a three-and-a-half-pound chicken and butcher it, leaving the wing and thigh bone intact. Preheat a sauté pan on high heat and add canola oil, just a scant amount, enough to coat the pan. When the oil starts to smoke, pat the chicken dry with a paper towel, then season with salt and pepper. Place it in the pan, skin side down. Next, take a brick from any convenient construction site, wrap it in foil, and place it on the chicken, allowing no air space between the skin and the surface of the blazing pan. Hoist the whole heavy mess and throw in the oven on as high a temperature as it will go. Blast it for twelve minutes or so until it is cooked. The bird will be crispy brown to perfection. Flip the pretty side up and present on wood-grilled portobello mushrooms. Done. We jazzed up the Thai calamari salad with serrano chilis and a soy-and-lime-based vinaigrette, and reinvented the infamous whole snapper from my smoke-filled kitchen on East 9th Street— this time with adequate ventilation. For the meat and potatoes crowd, we did a Porterhouse steak for two, and if that was not heart attack enough, added a runny Cambozola cheese sauce over the twice-baked potatoes. Jon and I cooked these and a bunch more simple dishes for the owners' friends and family and they loved it. It was a good test run. The vibe was right and summer was barreling in. I could almost do no wrong.

We opened on a warm, sweet spring weekend with this incredibly accessible menu, nothing unfamiliar or scary on it. You could order a local breast of duck, or lobster, flounder, or scallops. The food was elegant and simple, and lo and behold, the people came. The *New York Times* even weighed in, which might have been a first for this location, and their generous words instantly made us a must-stop destination on the Montauk Highway. The recognition was terrific, but all of a sudden our gentle summer vanished. We had just over a hundred seats and we were packed seven nights a week. We loaded up on waitstaff, added an extra bartender and some local talent to help in the kitchen, and we were jamming.

Jon and I were complete opposites in personality. Back then I tended to be pretty calm and always looked to smooth things over. I hated confrontation. I think I still carried some of my old habits from the early days when staying employed seemed the long view of my reasonable goals. Jon, on the other hand, didn't give a shit about what anyone thought of him, and I really admired him for this. He had rented out the extra room in the house with me and Amy, so we were roommates and family and workmates for a little while until he got settled.

One morning we were at the local grocery store stocking up the house on food and necessities when we encountered this awful, obnoxious, alarmingly tan woman cutting all sorts of people off in line and making a terrible ruckus. Jon, Mr. Justice for All, was watching her and I could tell he was getting worked up. She finally came up behind us and said, "Excuse me sir, can you reach that roll of toilet paper on the top shelf for me?" Jon turns and says, "No. As a matter of fact, I can't. I've been watching you for the last ten minutes and you've been rude to every person in this store. Not a chance, lady. Get it yourself." Applause broke out.

Jon was a kick hamming it up in public, but he was occasionally a problem in the kitchen. When one of our cooks burned a lamb loin by accident one night, Jon roasted the poor guy's ass so badly that the kid went scurrying back to the LIRR station and caught the next train home to wherever he had come from. The talent pool in the Hamptons was very limited, and we couldn't afford to be firing cooks. We had to pick up the slack. So I learned to be more forceful and Jon even managed to rope it in on occasion. We were running a hot place and I could hardly complain.

The season came to an end and for the first time in I don't know how long, I had this pervasive and foreign sense of being content. Amy and I were doing great, and after the debacle I had created in my marriage, I was relieved to not find myself looking at other women. So this was how other people did it? We hung out with all my old friends from the Nick & Toni's days. Oceans stayed open and popular in the off-season, but only on weekends, so my plate was full but not insane. It was just the right amount of work and I was able to really enjoy something that resembled a normal life for the first time since I originally picked up a sauté pan.

That Thanksgiving Amy and I had my parents and my brother and his wife out for a fabulous turkey dinner. I was living in a real house in East Hampton with a screen door and a fireplace, and my mother couldn't have been happier. Amy was easygoing and sweet with my parents, which was especially nice because the divorce had been hard on them. My dad had run into my former in-laws at our local hometown bakery shortly after all the drama ceased. Gina's mother saw my dad, made some disparaging comments to people waiting in line for Kaiser rolls, and then went off, nearly clocking him with a loaf of warm marble rye right out of the oven. Our lack of drama was a great relief to them. My mom hadn't even asked me if I was nuts or when I was going to settle down and start acting like an adult. I think that was because there was a distinct possibility I had finally become one.

It was good to be out of the city. I wasn't being seduced by the behavior that had landed me in such hot water in the first place. Amy had taken a part-time job at a local nursery and that kept her just busy enough. The winter days on eastern Long Island were gray and rainy and cold, and we rented movies and listened to old CDs. Had that winter never ended, we might have coasted indefinitely in domestic bliss. But the Hamptons is an intensely seasonal place, and sure enough, when the new season heated up, the changes caught up to us.

There was a local joint for rent across the street from Oceans, and Jerry could not leave well enough alone. He snapped it up just prior to the hot season and handed it to Jon to take over as chef. Just like that, Jerry had two businesses, separated by a double yellow traffic line, and they were poaching profits from each other.

Meanwhile, the rent on our idyllic East Hampton hideaway doubled and we had to move out to a rented floor in an old Sag Harbor colonial, a few towns down the highway. Amy, who had grown restless sitting home waiting to meet me night after night once the season kicked in, took a job as bartender at a tacky East End nightclub. I shouldn't have been surprised. This latest career move on her part was hardly out of character. Still, no one had schooled me on the rules for dating bartenders. One night when I arrived there at three a.m. to pick her up I was a little disturbed to find her in a skimpy halter-top behind the bar entertaining a male audience that was four deep. I ran back to my car and grabbed her a waffled long-john shirt and fought my way through the sea of men wondering how I ended up on the set of *Saturday Night Fever*. I handed her the long-sleeved shirt across the bar and she glared at me and said, "What the hell is this?" No one looked better than her in a halter-top, and here I was trying to diminish her ability to rake in tips. I slunk home and took her wrath when she returned that night. I deserved it. A week later she quit her bartending post and took a job in retail, which probably was not the best move financially but, I'll admit, did keep my blood pressure in check.

Even with the competition across the street, we had a decent summer at Oceans. However, once the season was over things took a turn for the worse. Business dropped off and the team of investors vanished back to the city and we were letting cooks go and checks were starting to bounce all over the beach. I had seen this show before.

All summer we had been getting our produce from an outfit called Anthony & Co. We were buying tens of thousands of dollars of fruit and vegetables from a guy named Tony, who I assumed was the proprietor because he took the orders over the phone and delivered them himself. Tony was soft-spoken, six-feet plus, and about threee hundred pounds. He wore his Bronx accent proudly and he and I got along great. When the checks started bouncing, he pulled me aside one day and said, "Johnny, doo-me-a-fayvuh. Before I tro' dis stool troo da window, maybe you can getcha boss to settle up deez bills. I mean, I'm in for ten large."

I've seen *The Godfather* about a hundred times and I'm an impressionable kid and it was a no-brainer. If Tony wanted the ten grand we owed him, I wanted him to have it. I went upstairs to the office and relayed the message. Jerry wrote a check on the spot. I noticed his hand was shaking a little as he signed. I delivered the check to Tony, who assured me that "if dis check bounces, I'll be back to rip dis place apart with my bare hands. No offense, Johnny. You I love." I believed him on both counts. It seemed like the time had come to move on.

Amy and I were both ready, too. Our country honeymoon was over. We'd seen every movie in the East Hampton Video Shop and many of our local friends had jumped ship. We took a small place in the city that my brother was giving up. Back in New York, my restaurant impresario friend and former boss Dan Benson had his empire going full tilt and he agreed to meet with me.

The last days of summer dwindled. Amy, back in June, had planted this amazing garden in a sunny patch we commandeered on the side of our Sag Harbor house. I should have guessed that my girlfriend would have had a green thumb, given her Midwestern roots. The week before we packed up in October she reaped a tremendous harvest of tomatoes and peppers and summer squash and buckets of fresh herbs.


On moving day, a major October nor'easter slammed into Sag Harbor. We loaded up the Beamer in the slashing rain but the movers were nowhere in sight. I had a meeting set up that evening with Dan Benson, and he was expecting me before the dinner crush. Amy told me to go—she'd handle the move herself. I kissed her in the driving rain and ducked into the car. The last thing I saw as I drove away was the remnants of her garden washing away in a muddy stream, as the snarled chicken wire she had so lovingly installed to keep out the rabbits flapped in the gusting wind.

# More Butter

The Waverly Inn was finally starting to take shape. A team of construction workers, under the watchful eye of Emil, were shoring up walls and refinishing the old rough-hewn floors and adding soundproofing and paint to the low ceilings. High-gloss white subway tiles from floor to ceiling gave the kitchen an almost sanitary feel, and the brand-new shimmering stainless-steel ranges that had arrived had us foaming at the bit. Once we got those beasts hooked up to the gas, we'd be up for some serious shit.

I was sweeping up one morning behind a tangle of old refrigeration pipes that were about to go, when I unearthed a stack of yellowing menus jammed between the floorboards. My suspicion was that they had served as a hole-stopper to keep out whatever was trying to get in, maybe twenty or more years ago. They looked timeless, printed on paper stock that was an inch thick, back when that kind of waste was not ecologically incorrect. I opened one out of curiosity. What a snapshot to a previous era of eating. Meat loaf. Oysters. Steak. Chicken Potpie. Barely a word of description. All of a sudden, three months of searching and speculation and ambivalence about what the Waverly food would be came to an end for me. This uncluttered simple menu captured the spirit of the place perfectly. We'd do the same kind of food they had done in the heyday, only updated, lighter, and healthier. Better. This was going to be my chance to put my best chef foot forward. At last I was inspired.

The old Waverly had a broiled pork chop on the menu that was certainly a no-brainer. It got me thinking about pork belly, back then the oft-forgotten, utterly delicious cut used mostly for bacon. So I got a side of the best Berkshire pork belly, known for its distinctive English heritage going back three hundred years. I cured it for twenty-four hours in peppercorns, juniper berries, and a mix of kosher salt and sugar and herbs. I cooked it at a very low temperature until it came out with the texture of a stick of butter. I cut it into perfect three-quarter-inch cubes and served it with bright green mizuna leaves. (Nine out of ten customers can't identify mizuna, but chefs love this kind of stuff—anything not found in Waldbaum's or Safeway, or is seasonal and only around for a short time—that is what we live for. If I can get it and you can't, I win. Even if the product is indistinguishable from a dozen other vegetables. That's the chef game.)

The result of my pork belly experiment? Perfect. Delicious. At least I thought so. The partners, on the other hand, weren't wild for it. Too fatty and too unhealthy for the general populace. Plus there were actresses to think about and the camera adding ten pounds, which may not be an issue for everyone, but when your partners both come from L.A., it counts. "Keep going, Chef" was the encouraging battle cry.

Disappointed, yet empowered, I decided to flex my chef muscles and take on marrow bones. The idea of scooping out the unctuous marrow with a bulalo spoon (yes, there actually is a specific tool that serves no other purpose than to scoop marrow out of bones) and smearing it onto grilled charred crispy sourdough was intensely appealing to me. How many times had I enjoyed that very same guilty pleasure at Blue

Ribbon, a SoHo institution famous for having a predominant number of chefs slurping marrow out of veal bones at four a.m. The guys at Blue Ribbon had perfected the ideal glutinous snack.

So I rustled up a slew of bones and scrubbed them clean as a whistle with an iron mesh brush. I roasted them with some foil on the ends so the marrow wouldn't run out, serving them up alongside a bed of beluga lentils cooked with a little minced shallot and hunks of carrot, celery, and onion accompanied with some grilled slices of sourdough. The look of disdain from Eric and Sean and the rest of the group answered that day's work in a heartbeat. "Too gnarly, dude" was becoming a familiar refrain.

There were other flops. It was humbling, yet ultimately good for me. All of America was up in arms over the foie gras debate, so naturally I weighed in by scoring a rich, fat lobe of prime Hudson Valley goose liver. I ran it through a tami, which is basically a piece of fine mesh window screen stapled to a round, four-inch-thick cylinder of wood. Forcing a malleable substance through the fine mesh breaks down the texture to a silky puree in a way that a blender or food processor could never hope to do. Once the foie gras had passed through the tami, I rolled it into a perfect cylinder in cheesecloth and cured it with sugar and spices and herbs and a touch of cayenne. I let it sit for three days, took it out of the curing mixture, and hung it like a prosciutto in the walk-in box for several more days. When I deemed it done and hard to the touch, I sliced it as precisely as a surgeon and served it with toast points, cornichons, and a little macerated fruit. Again, the coalition declared a resounding no. At least this gallant effort sparked a colorful, heartfelt debate between Eric and some invited guests who had joined for the tasting. I was utterly entertained, listening from the kitchen.

Night after night, Sean, Eric, Graydon, Emil, and friends would come in for tasting dinners, and the menu finally started to take shape—

simple, clean, and pristine—but with my touch added to the dishes from the stack of old menus I had unearthed. The failed marrow and foie gras gave way to a winning roast chicken, a Dover sole, and a cedar-plank trout. I had always been intrigued with cooking with wood. The aroma and dry intense heat make everything taste and smell better. I got hold of some cedar planks at a lumberyard near the restaurant and started to experiment. Keeping the American theme in mind, I procured some rainbow trout and boned it out. I soaked the planks in water and placed the butterflied fish on the plank head. Then I put the whole thing under the salamander, which is a broilerlike contraption with its intense heat source emanating from above. The smell of the burning wood wafted through the kitchen, out to the dining room, and into the very soul of the trout. Menu item done.

One afternoon I was noodling around with some new ideas in the kitchen when one of our cooks mentioned there was someone out front. I went to explore. A distinguished-looking woman was poking around the place without any seeming purpose. I greeted her pleasantly enough and she immediately started asking questions. Who is the chef? Is this going to be some fancy place? What's the menu like? She told me about the history of the old Waverly Inn and seemed to know all about Graydon and was cautiously skeptical about what this place was about to become. She obviously knew a lot more than I did about almost everything. She knew an awful lot about food, too. Finally, as she was getting ready to leave, out of the blue she announces, "You know what? You need to have biscuits here."

"OK," I said cordially enough. Just what I needed, more opinions about what the food should be. "By the way, who are you?" I asked as politely as I could.

"Mimi. Mimi Sheraton."

I have spent half my life enjoying the work of this highly respected writer and former *New York Times* food critic, and she has just announced to me that we need biscuits. Why would anyone in New York want a biscuit? And what business does a guy from Brooklyn have making them? All I could initially think was what a pain in the ass it would be. They'd have to be cooked fresh every twenty minutes, and where? Our kitchen was barely big enough to do the 150 dinners we projected in the first place. Maybe I shouldn't even experiment, I thought. If they were any good, the partners would never give me the option of saying no. On the other hand, who was I to argue with Mimi Sheraton?

I turned to my chef friend Love (yes, that is really her name), who told me she had a bona fide Southern grandmother, or at least she hailed from South Jersey. Either way, she had a recipe for authentic biscuits that I shamelessly cribbed. There is just something about the confluence of butter, flour, and a little sugar that makes normal people irrational. You would have thought I grew up saying "y'all" and not "youse guys," based on the response I got. The biscuits were a go. Same for the whole Dorade baked in rosemary and sea salt, as well as a traditional chicken potpie.

There was still the matter of what we'd do for desserts. At this stage of the game we had no budget for a pastry chef, so I started pulling recipes out of thin air. I mean, I couldn't very well put out all this exciting food and then tell everyone to mosey over to Magnolia Bakery to wait on line for a cupcake. Coming up with a workable dessert menu turned out to be a lot more daunting than I anticipated. Baking is an exacting scientific endeavor. No "a pinch of this and a splash of that." Baking is classical music compared to savory cooking's jazz. My demeanor and very nature is contrary to the discipline needed for baking. There is no improvising or syncopated back beats. One cup equals one cup. A little more of this or that is disastrous to the outcome of the recipe. Still, we needed something on the menu, so I took a conservative approach, nothing crazy—apple crisps, peach cobblers. I even tried Bananas Foster, the old fifties standby. I also fiddled with a chèvre cheesecake until I got the balance of sweet and tart just right.

Ultimately, I hired Lidia, a pastry chef I had worked with in the past. She took my simple ideas and executed them perfectly and brought them to a whole new level. The partners were especially taken by the Bananas Foster and thought it would be fun to do a little old-school flambé at the table. I think I did it tableside once and nearly singed off my eyelashes, not to mention some very intricate appliqué work on the dress of the woman who had ordered it. We made it in the kitchen from then on.

The menu was really shaping up, but we were sorely lacking in greens, or as one of the partners would say, "chick food." Honestly, I had not given it a ton of thought. But Eric and Sean—two native Californians, had. And the consensus was, there was no better salad than the one served at The Ivy in L.A.

I'd eaten the famous Ivy salad before. I thought I remembered it well, so in an effort to satisfy the powers that be, I re-created the West Coast industry standard—only, in my mind, better. The key ingredients were the smoky mesquite-grilled vegetables. We did not have the luxury of a mesquite wood–burning grill in the tiny Waverly kitchen, so I would have to improvise. I went to the Bowery on the Lower East Side and scored a stovetop smoker and some mesquite chips. I cold-smoked plates full of zucchini and yellow squash and asparagus and corn. Then I grilled them perfectly, with beautiful hatch marks, diced them up, and whipped up a zesty lemon vinaigrette—lemon juice, some Dijon, minced shallots, and olive oil. I did this all on the sly and laid it out for the guys the next afternoon, plated beautifully and without a word of fanfare. Sean took one look and without even lifting his fork to taste it, reached for his cell phone. "Hey, Stayce," he said to his manager in L.A. "Go over to The Ivy, will ya, and FedEx me 'the' salad. Thanks." I guess it was my expression that said, Yo, what about my laboriously prepared effort?

His clearly vocal reply was, "Dude, that's not it."

* * *

The next day a FedEx package arrived with a to-go container of wilted greens and soggy vegetables. I got out three forks and we sat there eating day-old salad. I wasn't blown away, but they were happy, so I devised a reasonable facsimile, which we now call Waverly Grilled Vegetable Salad.

Amazingly, thirteen months had gone by since our first meeting in the paint and sawdust with Graydon, and still we were not open. Thirteen months of construction and permit delays, failed and postponed inspections, changes of heart about paint colors and fixtures and lightbulbs. The gas company wouldn't turn on the gas for our new ranges because it needed some paperwork that no one knew about or had even heard of, so now we were forced to finalize the menu by cooking on a $249 porcelain electric stove that Emil brought in. The stove featured two sorry-ass coil-type burners that could barely boil a pot of water after fifteen minutes. That's the way it was going those last weeks. Tempers were coming to a boil faster than any stocks I was doing.

Through all of this, we were paying out salaries to all sorts of kitchen staff. Those of us who had even a small partner share were not sharing in anything but headache, lost wages, and allergic reactions to construction dust. Under Emil's critical eye, and Sean and Eric's vision, we had built a restaurant. We had a menu and a kitchen for me to work in. We had a cellar full of wine and a sous chef and three cooks and waiters and a hostess and someone to take reservations. It was all there, except for one thing. We still weren't in business.

By now, word on the street was deafening that Graydon Carter, literary lion, was about to roam in a whole new jungle. *New York* magazine had done an uninformed teaser piece on us, and somehow got hold of my cell phone number and now wanted the exclusive. Food bloggers were circling like vultures over carrion, and even the *Times* had given us a small mention. It was becoming a feeding frenzy, but we weren't offering up a single morsel. Finally, one day, Sean, ostensibly tired of writing checks, threw down his cell phone and announced, "That's it. We're opening on Thursday."

"But we don't even have a listed telephone number yet," I pointed out.

"Dude, we're opening."

We set up an e-mail address and gave Graydon the heads-up. We printed the menus on the office copier and put the word "Preview" on them so that there'd be no mistake that this was anything but a test run. We were going to open soft and keep it low-key. Maybe some people would come. Maybe, with any luck, the press wouldn't notice. It was our hope that we could fly under the radar until we worked the kinks out. We had no choice. It was time. We opened our doors at six p.m. on a Thursday night with no phones, no reservations, and a menu billed as "preview." And we waited to see what would happen.

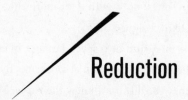

# Reduction

With Oceans and our Bridgehampton experience fading fast, Amy and I were both happy to be back in the city. We set up shop in our tiny one bedroom in a West Village elevator building. The place looked out on Greenwich Street, a block from the Hudson River. The building had decent old bones, though the apartment was lacking in style, having been updated to that seventies tenement white-paint-and-plasterboard look with cheap cabinets and questionable plumbing and clanking radiator pipes. Still, the old puffy popsicle-colored sofa fit like a dream and we were happy to be home.

My reunion with Dan Benson was promising. His empire had quadrupled in size since I last saw him a year ago. He remained a master at offering up delicious, approachable food in a popular of-the-moment ambience, and his restaurants were all going gangbusters. His latest project was to be called Dockside, the kind of Upper East Side food factory complete with sushi bar that I'd normally do anything to avoid—as a patron, for sure. Still, I respected Dan's work ethic and, what's more, he was dangling a separate new opportunity in front of me if I decided to come aboard. As if not leveraged enough, he was conspiring to do a rustic Italian restaurant downtown just off West Broadway in SoHo.

The huge space was tied up in some sort of elaborate real estate shenanigans, but knowing him, I just assumed, as always, that he had the upper hand in the deal and would have it locked up within a few months. His plan was to knock off Nick & Toni's, only with a lot more chicken. So when he asked me to get on board, I signed on.

Clearly I had earned some modicum of respect, because in essence, Dan asked me to help open the kitchen operation at Dockside. By now I had done this enough times that you'd think I knew the ropes. My first day, I was attempting to light a faulty pilot on the brand-new Viking range. I put my head in the oven with a blowtorch borrowed from one of the plumbers and fired it up. The next thing I know, *BOOM*, I'm on my ass, the proud owner of a first-degree burn, all my eyelashes and eyebrows gone. The embarrassment shook me up far worse than the injuries.

Dan had his own vision for the look and feel of his restaurants, and as a veteran I understood this mandate. A House of Benson was not the place to try new things. I knew how to "get the food out of the kitchen," and Dan knew I did, too. The process at Dockside bore an uncanny resemblance to what we went through back in the Park South days. The only difference was that Dan now had a team of food consultants on the payroll—ex-chefs, ex–food writers, and trusted friends of the boss with occasionally useful, but mostly annoying opinions, who were using their experience to capitalize on the early-nineties restaurant boom. They were hired ostensibly to prove the chefs wrong. "Try this with that," they'd command, though never actually close enough to any chef near a hot pan that might be effective as a weapon. "This doesn't work—more seasoning," they'd write in their tasting notes. The consultants were paid to be critical, so if they aren't critical, how can they justify their existence? At least Dan no longer needed to run through each of his places asking 175 diners how they liked their food.

In this supposedly streamlined environment, we developed a new tuna dish. There is an unwritten law in New York that says any person who willingly opens and operates a restaurant here must serve tuna fourteen ways, or at least as tartare, under penalty of being ignored by the food press and everyone living on the island of Manhattan. We came up with a version where you basically grill up a thick slab of tuna and garnish it with a veggie spring roll, finished with a rich veal stock–based sauce. For the spring roll you julienne a boatload of carrots and mushrooms, maybe a little daikon, and shreds of ginger. Sauté the whole mix in canola oil with a drop of sesame, cool the whole thing down and roll up several dozen in a thin spring-roll wrapper. Then pop it into the deep fryer for a minute or so until brown and crisp. You cut them on the bias and place atop each grilled tuna steak just before it goes out to the dining room. It was very appealing, with a nice texture and crunch to counteract the buttery character of the tuna.

I thought it was pretty good. The corporate chef thought it was pretty good. Even the Man himself "kinda liked it." The "experts" were called in for some real insight. We sweated it out as our hardworking team of food consultants tasted it for the final decision. Take the spring roll off. Taste it again. Put the spring roll back on. One more time. "Seems to have a deep-fried taste. Not recommended," one wrote in her notes. In the final tally, it passed. THANK GOD. Now there were only twenty-seven more menu items to go, not counting the sushi bar items. However, the Japanese sushi chefs were not subject to the same scrutiny as the rest of us. Not because of any cultural sensitivity, but because the moment the consultants start in, the sushi guys all lose their English language skills. Suddenly, according to the consultants, all the sushi dishes are just fine. "Quite delicious," in fact.

In addition to helping out at Dockside, I was designated a food spy for the corporation. My mere presence at one of the other locations would instill fear in the hearts of my fellow hardworking brethren. This made me uncomfortable, like I was on the wrong team—all answers but no investment in the product. After giving my spiel about a dish, I was gone. I flitted from restaurant to restaurant, testing recipes, making suggestions, helping oversee menus and food costs, and keeping heads hired and budgets in the black. My friend Jon had returned from the Hamptons and was running yet another Benson-led restaurant on the Upper West Side. He tolerated my presence only because, after working for me for a couple of years, he was conditioned to ignore me. And who could blame him. I had become a droning food bore. The chefs in the other joints were even less happy to see me. When I wasn't helping roll about five hundred spring rolls a day at Dockside, I was basically spying on my friends and neighbors. Frankly, my heart was not into it. When after a few months of this, Dan offhandedly mentioned that the deal for the Italian place had gone on hiatus for much longer than originally planned, I planned my exit strategy.

Andy Arons, one of the fifty-bucks-a-pop partners at Oceans, had run into me one day crossing the street near his office in SoHo. He had always been appreciative of my attention to detail, keeping the quality high and the costs in line. Although I would venture to say that he didn't see one dollar back on his investment, we still became friends. He was young and smart and operated a very successful chain of food stores. Andy had some involvement with the well-established, three-star-rated Voiage, the preeminent thalassic midtown eatery. He had learned that their chef was in a pinch. Billy, an Irish guy from South Jersey, had taken off into that ionosphere where chefs go to become media stars, spending more time on television or on the road cooking than in their own kitchens. They did it to raise their national profile, because despite the Food Channel–driven rock star image, restaurant chefs are not paid *that* much. What's more, with fewer restaurants offering insurance and retirement plans, it becomes prudent and just plain necessary to find additional income streams.

Billy's long-standing chef de cuisine, a decent guy who had ostensibly grown tired of being second banana, had finally landed his own gig and split on short notice. Billy was up the creek. He needed someone to run his kitchen while he tended to more pressing matters: media training sessions, photo shoots. My intuition told me I was all wrong for this gig, but Andy put in a good word anyway and, surprisingly, Billy asked me to meet him ASAP. The guy must have been desperate. All the same it was nice to be wanted by someone so high up the New York food chain at such a revered address. No one was going to Voiage to cruise the bar or have sex in the bathrooms. This was a different league.

I hauled up to Madison Avenue, a swanky part of midtown and perhaps the only neighborhood I'd less rather go to every day than the Upper East Side. I'd never been to Voiage before. I certainly couldn't afford to eat there. The place was decorated like a cruise ship, with gorgeous linen spread on every meticulously set table, along with the de rigueur elaborate china and crystal and opulent thick-handled silverware. I met with Billy in his office and he asked the usual questions in between fielding calls from agents and producers and journalists and PR reps. Without even putting the phone down, he invited Amy and me in for dinner to sample the menu.

I dusted off my old wedding suit for the occasion and Amy characteristically put on the lowest-cut, tightest dress she owned, with matching heels, which caused the mostly male dining clientele to collectively choke on their sturgeon osso buco and roast turbot with lemon buerre monte upon our arrival. I always enjoyed watching the affect she had on the male populace. That is, until I absolutely couldn't stand it.

Admittedly I had more than a little attitude and apprehension about this temporary visa into the gilded cooking class. I tend to get that way whenever I feel like I'm seeing my comfort zone in the rearview mirror. I suppose it is a defense mechanism. I'd had a great run at Oceans and it was gratifying to see myself written about in *USA Today* and the *New York Times*. No one was comparing me to the great French names who rack up stars in the Michelin guide, but still I was getting somewhere. Voiage, on the other hand, was a whole different level, and my professional fear of failure was at full tilt. Whatever I was thinking when we were seated, however, dissipated as soon as the food started coming.

We started with basil ravioli, then blackfish with a truffle vinaigrette. That was followed by lobster, turbot, and branzino. We were served plate after plate of delicate food and were plied with glasses of amazing whites and then three separate reds, one for each course. No expense was spared and it was impressive. This was very serious food served by serious waiters in a lovely ambience, though a trifle stiff.

I called Billy the next day to thank him, and he let me know that the job was mine. I gave Dan two weeks notice, pissing him off to no end. Ultimately, though, I think he understood the importance of having a place like this on my résumé. It was time to take some real risks. A few days before I was scheduled to start, I came down with a historic case of flu that was getting progressively worse. I was up all night Sunday throwing up and shivering. I was due at work at 7:00 a.m. Monday morning and there was no chance I was going to miss my first day, but Amy took one look at me crawling back from the toilet at dawn and told me I was not going anywhere. I figured if I could just buy a few hours of rest I'd be able to soldier through, so I called Billy at 6:00 a.m., then 6:15, 6:30. Finally, at 7:00 a.m., he answered his office phone and I told him I was so sorry but I was sick as a dog. Before I could get another word out, he said, "Fine, whatever," and hung up.

I dragged myself into work two days later, right on time at seven a.m. I was still so weak that I nearly passed out before I even put on my chef's jacket. Billy, who had assumed I was never going to show up in the first place, took one withering look at me and put me on a double shift the very first day. It was an auspicious start.

My main role as chef de cuisine was to manage the staff of cooks, and devise and set up the specials for lunch and dinner six days a week. That involved coming up with two or three ideas a day using absolutely the best ingredients money could buy. I'd start my morning with a shot of espresso and the faxes from our local purveyors to see what was fresh and available. The fish guy might have wild striper from Montauk, fresh tautog blackfish, head-off mahi mahi from Hawaii, softshell crab from Maryland, and Copper River salmon from Alaska. Then I'd check out my veggie guy's fax. He'd have spring root vegetables and arugula available, fresh field-cut mizuna and tatsoi, ramps, pencil leeks and baby Tokyo turnips, and twelve varieties of mushrooms: morels and black truffle and oyster and crimini and trumpet royals and whatever else was in season. From these daily communiqués I'd craft two or three specials, each unique to lunch and dinner, sometimes combining a larger order of an ingredient that especially interested me. I'd create three dishes from one order of say, forty pounds of fresh halibut, caught the day before twenty miles off the coast of Massachusetts.

On a typical Monday morning I might do an appetizer special of yellowtail flavored with hot oil seared and garnished with thinly sliced jalapeño, or razor clams from Long Island steamed in their own juices on the grill and then tossed with some black bean sauce. We'd drum these dishes up every morning and prep the ingredients and have the mise en place all set for the lunch crush right on time. Then Billy would stroll in a half hour before the first seating and take one look and decide NO, NO, NO and we'd all start from scratch. I think he was predisposed to hate everything I did. I never really got off the ground from that bad first week, and that was pretty much how I spent my days, playing catch-up for the food I created that he then shot down whenever he was around.

For months I suffered this humiliation, all the while trying to make my mark in the three-star world in which I'd been immersed. I was mostly about simplicity and fresh ingredients, but as in life, a bit un-fussy and maybe even a little lazy compared to the superstars of this world. (Do we really need to peel the tomatoes and the eggplant? My grandmother never did.) I'm sure it all looked good on the brave new world of The Food Channel, but I still couldn't see the value of hours spent brunoise-ing garlic. And don't even get me started on foam. I was born into and mostly bring a workingman's mentality to the kitchen, and maybe that was the problem.

Once, at Oceans, I was wolfing down an "everything" bagel on my way to work, dripping the tasty crumbs all over my clothes. I got to work and decided to experiment with a tuna loin. I rounded up some fresh herbs and poppy and sesame seeds and chopped some garlic and toasted up the whole mess with sea salt. I dipped a tuna loin into a bowl of beaten egg whites and rolled it in the herb mix and pan-fried it up, and it came out tangy and crunchy, and I thought, "Hmmm not bad. Everything tuna!" I put it on the menu as a special and it sold out before nine p.m. Simple, unfussy, and a huge hit.

Now, at Voiage I'm struggling for inspiration, tired to pieces, and I'm flat out of ideas. I decide to recycle the crusted tuna idea. I knew Billy would hate it, but frankly I was out of gas. I figured he'd come in the next day and shoot it down, cursing and screaming like he always did. I put in on the specials menu. He saw it, grunted, and let it go. A week later I'm reading the *Times* food section and there below the lower fold of the newspaper I see a picture of Billy with MY fucking tuna dish! The only thing I have been hearing from him for months is that I can't cook, and that's MY goddamned tuna with his soft-focus picture gloating over it, implying that it was perhaps his creation and not mine. It's not like you can copyright toasted sesame seeds, but still. Even my mother called to say, "John, isn't that the tuna dish you made for us out in the country?"

One week Billy disappeared for an especially long junket. Maybe it was "Celebrity Truffle Hunting with the Stars." He certainly seemed to be gone an awful lot lately, and there was a lot of whispering going on in the manager's office. Wow, I thought, if Billy was on his way out, this might be a really big break for me. I decided to visit with Henry, the executive director of services at Voiage. We chatted a bit about this and that and then I asked him point-blank: "Am I ever going to be the chef here?" The small talk vanished like a cloud of grease smoke up the exhaust hood. He said, "No, John. No chance. You don't have the pedigree. You don't have what it takes."

"How dare you, you sloppy two-faced, bad-haircut, baggy-suit motherfucker" is what I felt like saying. But in the end, I suppose he was as right as I was wrong for this job. I finished my lunch shift, went out on the street, and called Billy on his cell to tell him that after working fifteen-hour days, for six days a week, for nine months, I was resigning. As up shit's creek as he was about to become minus a chef yet again, he didn't even pause his incoming call that interrupted our heart to heart. "OK, buddy, I gotta take this call." I showed up for my final two weeks and worked with even more zeal, just to make the point, mostly to myself, that I had what it takes. Then I was gone. Never had I worked so hard to be so completely unappreciated.

# Piatti Secondi

Amy and I were married on an eye-poppingly gorgeous October day on the beach in Amagansett, Long Island. Two dozen members of our families along with our closest friends gathered under blue skies and near 80-degree temperatures. A local judge from Southampton presided over the ceremony on a makeshift altar crafted from some driftwood we found that had washed up onshore. My bride descended from the dunes walking barefoot through the sand in a lovely form-fitting designer wedding dress, looking very much like the cover of one of those thick glossy magazines. I took her hand in my second marriage dressed in a crisp new dark navy suit made just for the occasion. I looked like a skinny swarthy penguin.

The wedding party took place at Nick & Toni's in a huge tent set up in the backyard and generously provided for us by my old friend Jeff Salaway. My dad of course came through with the best ten-piece band on Long Island. And the Nick & Toni's kitchen drummed up a menu of everything the East End had to offer: platters of striped bass, local fresh oysters and clams, grilled white corn, steak, glorious end-of-season tomatoes, squash, zucchini, garden greens. Not to mention wheelbarrows of pasta for the Italian side of my family. What a mix of cultures came out to help us celebrate. We had cousins from Italy, new in-laws from the Midwest, favored acquaintances from Seattle and Staten Island and, of course, Brooklyn. We were surrounded by friends and family, nuns, cooks, lesbians, potheads, dishwashers, restaurant mavens, city folk, country bumpkins—all dancing and chattering well into the long, balmy, misty sea night. Amy and I flew to the Amalfi coast of Italy the next day, where we spent three weeks wandering from Sorrento to Positano to Salerno. Italian men, living up to their reputation, followed my wife everywhere she went. She racked up about three marriage proposals just walking to the corner *tabbacci* to get cigarettes. One young handsome Lothario even tried to bargain with me.

We dined at Don Alfonso 1890, a renowned restaurant set in the little backwoods village of Sant'Agata de' Goti. We had a meal that defies description, a mélange of local ingredients and exquisite olive oils and meats and cheeses and handmade pastas so delicate and fresh you could still see the Don's grandma's prints on them. Amazing as that feast was, though, it still didn't beat our lazy afternoons sitting on a giant volcanic rock looking out on the Bay of Naples with a chunk of chewy focaccia-like bread we found in a little bakery with a wood-burning stone oven so old that it looked like it predated the Renaissance. Next door there was a quaint *salumeria* where we picked up the most luscious mozzarella made by hand right there, still warm in a giant glass jar on the counter. We'd buy a basket of tomatoes from a tiny open market in front of this gorgeously decrepit church and we were set. I had never dreamed I'd tie the knot again, but dozing off with Amy in a wine-soaked haze with the hot Italian sun kissing my nose, it was hard to imagine better. We had about a thousand bucks in the bank and I owed two for the rent, but on that day I felt I was a very wealthy man.

But since conjugal bliss was not paying the bills, it was on me to put Voiage behind me and find something that was not just another job. The formula behind a successful restaurant sometimes defies any sense of logic or business acumen. There are owners who enjoy food and enjoy people and have an uncanny sense for marrying the two. The best understand the successful mix of menu, ambience, and razor-sharp cost management. Were it that easy, however, everyone would be in the food business. More often than not, though, it was a far more eclectic and passion-driven set of circumstances that led to the opening of a new place. In the case of Colina, where I landed, it was a containership full of barn wood from Brazil.

The man who started Colina, Dave Tipton, was an owner in a New York landmark store that specialized in the universe's largest collection of carpets, as well as four floors of furniture and bric-a-brac collected from every corner of the globe. It is hard to be a New Yorker and not have set foot in this place at least once. A Hamptons summer resident, Dave was a regular at Nick & Toni's and had befriended Jeff Salaway. The two had even talked about doing a restaurant together someday. As it turned out, Dave had a vast empty space attached to his flagship store off lower Broadway. He had just bought up this enormous supply of beautiful, rough-hewn wood and beams that had gone from one life as old barn board in Brazil to a second life as a country restaurant, and then, finally, ended up being deconstructed and loaded into a shipping container to make its way to a side-street service entrance in New York City. Dave got Jeff on board, cleared out valuable retail space in his store, and Colina went from pipe dream to reality.

The new partners in crime brought in the legendary Jonathan Waxman as chef to design the culinary end of their enterprise. Jonathan came to New York in the early 1980s, a young chef who had introduced California cuisine to the city at a restaurant called Jams. Wildly successful and just plain wild, he lived a page out of *Bright Lights, Big City*. He opened and then closed a couple more restaurants, ferrying between places in his vintage Ferrari. His food could best described as a hybrid of France and California; laid back, simple, and unfussy but with masterful technique. I related to him very organically because he was also a musician, playing the trombone well enough to gig with rock bands and orchestras in an earlier chapter of his life. Jams flamed out along with the economy in the late 1980s, and Jonathan sold his Ferrari and lived off the proceeds for several years on the West Coast, until the temptations of New York beckoned him back to the scene. The partners also poached a fabulous pastry chef, Patty Jackson, who had cut her teeth with the legendary restaurateur and entrepreneur Pino Luongo, whose restaurants Le Madri, Coco Pazzo, and Tuscan Square are responsible in large part for bringing a Tuscan sensibility to New York City. I was brought in to run the kitchen and, frankly, after my Voiage experience I would have happily run the hot-dog concession at The Garden. Besides, I loved Jeff and would have done anything for him—including getting on board at yet another restaurant in its infancy.

I had no problem working under the tutelage of Jonathan Waxman. He was the kind of chef you wanted to be aligned with. Not long after we were introduced, I was just getting down to work one day when he tapped me on the shoulder and simply said, "Follow me." We walked out of the kitchen, through the entire length of the restaurant and straight out the door. The whole time he didn't say a word. On the street we walked half a block to a dive bar where two ice-cold martinis sat on a small table awaiting our arrival. He nodded a thank-you to the bartender as we took our seats. "Johnny," he said raising his glass. "Sometimes you just have to stop and have a drink."

Jonathan was renowned for being a quirky genius who could work complex miracles with the simplest of ingredients. He coerced the owners to outfit the Colina kitchen with both a wood-fired rotisserie spit roaster and a wood-burning pizza oven, much like the one at Nick & Toni's, which fast became the restaurant's centerpiece. Jonathan would take a baby lamb and get it going on the spit, turning all day long. It smelled like heaven, the lamb juices basting inside and the skin turning crackled with just a little garlic, olive oil, herbs, and salt. I'd look at that rotating spit and I'd say, "Chef, what do we do now?" And he'd respond, "Nothing, nothing. Don't do a thing, Johnny." That was his philosophy with almost everything he prepared, and one I would gladly adopt.

Meanwhile, Patty was turning out fresh, crispy grissini and excellent focaccia and incredibly luscious desserts: lovingly wrought *pana cotta* and cannoli and tiramisu, adding one more layer of credibility to the menu. I was making fresh pastas and perfecting wood-fired pizzas to contribute to the mix. The artisans who did the finish on the barn boards made the whole place look and feel like you had just walked into a Tuscan farmer's very elegant personal barn.

There is one intangible that haunts anyone who has any experience in the restaurant business, and it is as simple as the cooking I was doing. You can build and design and spend on the details and hire talent and do tasting menu after tasting menu and come up with a surefire winner. But you cannot guarantee that anyone will get it. We opened our doors and the people came. They simply did not come back. Maybe it was the odd entrance on a side street that forced people to almost detour their way in. Maybe it was the low-hung beam ceilings, so out of place in New York: This was the very wood that inspired the construction of Colina in the first place. Or perhaps people just did not want to eat in a carpet store. One thing is for sure. The scathing *New York Times* review did not help. It was bad enough that they did not get the food. But they even took exception to our barn board.

Jonathan, with Jeff's blessing, had designed an innovative menu that featured a limited selection of the freshest ingredients, and you had no more than a handful of choices to make. It was not unlike the country-style home restaurant that works all over Italy, where you walk into a place on a side street in Rome or Milan or Florence and you're seated and fed pretty much what the chef feels like cooking that day—a meal that leaves you weeping tears of gratitude. Colina was after the same effect. We set out to be a simple place where you could share the chef's finest handiwork in a casual setting, with other aficionados hungry for elegant simple fare. It was heartbreaking on so many levels to see it all go awry. We had poured so much love and sweat and tears into the place. And the great irony was that Jeff and Jonathan's food vision was right on the money, only about a half-dozen years too early. While some restaurateurs were ruling by committee, these owners followed a different calling. Gut instinct versus consensus. In the end, their gut lost out.

The death spiral was fast and final. I'd seen it all before—the layoffs, the cutbacks, the unpaid bills. Colina had been born of two men's visions and died with barely a whimper. I was back out on the street, and now the street was a large apartment on West 87th that we took in order to spread out. Amy had taken a day job in a women's cosmetic shop at 80th and Madison. From our triumphant return to New York and new jobs and Greenwich Village, we had somehow ended up living on a clerk's wages on the Upper West Side. It was as far away as I could imagine from where we wanted or expected to be.

I kissed Amy good-bye every morning and watched her jump on the 86th Street crosstown bus to go to work with New York's blue-haired elite. I searched in vain for a decent espresso anywhere north of Times Square. When we had chosen our new place in the Art Deco building, we had visions of grandeur. We fancied ourselves leading characters in a stage play of domestic bliss. Sadly, it all proved to be an illusion. Instead of raucous, wine-soaked dinner parties with our visiting downtown friends, I spent the bulk of my time dodging women in old college sweatshirts pushing double strollers on Broadway. It was a scene that only changed at dusk when their husbands came home from work and took over stroller patrol in their pleated Dockers and Topsiders. I occasionally rode my bicycle to Riverside Park over by the Hudson River out of sheer boredom. There were like all of thirty boats at the 79th Street Boat Basin. Why on earth did so many men on the Upper West Side own Topsiders? It was not a question I wanted to be contemplating.

# The Man

Golf can make you rich. This must be true, because everyone I know who has some kind of equity position in a restaurant tees off at the crack of dawn at one of those idyllic, manicured country clubs where the dues eclipse the annual GNP of a small Latin American country. Precious few of *my* conversations include the phrase "five iron" in them. Maybe I need to do something about that, because when my Bridgehampton benefactor and investor friend Andy called to tell me about his golf weekend, it landed me an introduction to Emmanuel Stern.

Emmanuel was an Old Testament New York real estate mogul who had upset the protected climes of Manhattan's historic SoHo district by building the first new large-scale hotel in nearly a hundred years. After a brief and congenial telephone conversation, Emmanuel put me in touch with the person who could get me in touch with his people. That was my "in" to the Grand, which had quietly opened to great popularity in 1999. Now Stern was in the final phases of construction on the Grand's sister edifice, one block south. This translated to a whole lot of cooking that was needed.

The Grand was all lobby and glass and concrete and bar space—ostensibly built to fit the architecture of the landmark neighborhood.

However, critics saw it more as an L.A. movie star hangout transported to the fringe streets of what was left of industrial downtown Manhattan. Just being greeted by *any* open space in New York was unusual. Finding yourself in a wide open plain of marble floors with custom-made aluminum furniture and a bar glistening with exotic jade bottles was like stumbling into an alternative pseudo-hip universe. All those empty bar tables were crying out for someone to bring some zip to the menu. Maybe I was just the man for the job.

I met with the director of food and beverage, a strikingly handsome, youngish blond-haired guy named Donald. He was hard to miss with his goofy, clunky, black-framed glasses, no doubt from the Allan Mikli boutique sample sale I had passed on the way in. Was there even glass in those frames? I wasn't so sure. Donald had migrated from some Midtown food palace, and once south of 14th Street, traded up for black pants, a black jacket, black shirt, and black square-toed shoes. I resisted the urge to ask about the glasses, and once I got past his choice of eyewear we had a great conversation. He truly seemed to have an interest in doing something with that huge lobby bar space. The hotel also had a small out-of-the-way restaurant that desperately needed some love and attention to put it on the map. There had been talk of converting it from Continental food to an intimate Italian spot. I could already imagine the wood-burning oven, some simple pasta dishes and plainly grilled fish. I could dream, after all.

Despite my initial skepticism, I was pleased that Donald seemed to like my ideas. He had this habit of nodding his head as if to agree with everything, and you wanted him to. He was like the high school quarterback you befriended because wherever he went, you knew there would be great parties and cute girls. With his blessing I was quickly pushed up the hiring ladder.

I interviewed with managers from accounting, room sales, and human resources. I met the vice president of the Committee of New

Hires, and the head of security—a barrel-chested ex-cop in a black suit similar to Donald's. They must have been giving them away as part of the employment contract, I thought with trepidation. I met the head of information technology, concierge services, room service, and house-keeping. They had a vice president for just about everything here, and when I thought I couldn't force another smile, I had to go through a final review meeting with the entire cast in a boardroom crammed so full you couldn't fit in another chair. I was grilled by the head of accounting, who wanted to know how fast I could get Food & Beverage bottom-line numbers to her if we did, say, a midweek roast duck special. I asked her what day she preferred to eat duck. Fortunately, after a very awkward pause, the entire committee burst out laughing.

I survived death-by-boardroom and was eventually led to a top-floor executive suite where I had a brief audience with the CEO, who had an extensive down-tempo electronica CD collection lining the entire wall of his office. While we spoke, an intoxicating, funky beat played throughout the interview on this very mod-looking stereo console. I could barely concentrate during our talk because that music was so hypnotic, and I think I agreed to a lower salary than I should have, but what the hell? I was having a good time and he had some rare London import CDs that he offered to let me borrow if I got the job. He put out a memo to the seven underlings that I'd interviewed with, to say that I was invited to do a tasting demonstration. It seemed like a lot of trouble to go through for a job that I didn't even know if I wanted, but the rent was due. So I came in and did a lobster risotto, some crab cakes, and a crispy chicken.

Donald informed me that I had the job. Then he gave me a sheaf of documents thicker than my divorce papers. I had to review the contract and sign the Hotel Employee Bill of Rights. The place had more policies than I had good ideas. Be nice to guests, no touching your nose or hair in the public spaces. Never use the front elevators in uniform. It was starting to feel like I was enlisting instead of accepting a job, but there were pluses, too. I had vacation days, sick time, flex time, health insurance, and a retirement account—all things unheard of in the restaurant world I had come from. Maybe this hotel business wasn't such a bad idea after all.

My official mandate was to ramp up the bar menu to something that was more than a bar menu. I scheduled tasting after tasting, which the entire boardroom committee was invited to attend. I was pulling recipes out of my ass to come up with something, anything that could pass as potential bar food: mini crab cakes, mini crumpets with caviar, mini lobster risotto cakes. I probably should have been more concerned that the head of security thought my crab cakes needed more cilantro, but the place was not really geared toward food. It was mostly geared toward pastel-colored drinks with silly names that are fun to order when intoxicated. I had the sinking feeling that no one really cared what I did in the kitchen as long as the tropical fruit–infused vodka was flowing. I had benefits, a salary, and a 401(k), same as every other manager. No one was taking any big chances at bucking the system at the Grand. Why should I rock the culinary boat?

I brought in my talented friend Missy to serve as sous chef. She was a serious cook with an Ivy League education and an impressive food pedigree. While Donald was busy putting out fires, I struck up a fast friendship with his food and beverage manager, Emily, a young woman of Czech descent with a monstrous work ethic. She and Missy hit it off and the three of us became great friends—a triumvirate united against the machine. We worked endless hours trying desperately to bring some sense of levity to the uptight corporate, micromanaged environs. Donald, meanwhile, was fielding tense executive-suite meetings about how the Grand was going to turn its food and beverage program around.

One afternoon he came down to inform us that a major change was afoot. First of all, management was no longer supporting the tiny upstairs restaurant. There'd be no Italian place any time soon. However, they were very committed to upgrading the presentation in the lounge area and turning it into a bona fide downtown destination. I had my doubts, but Donald seemed pumped up. They had just completed a two-hour brainstorming session that I could only imagine, and they'd come up with *the* concept. We were going to do "tiers" of food. They had even procured these iron three-tiered serving stands. My commission was to create something to go on them, like crab, shrimp, and chicken. Or beef brochettes, perhaps. We could, Donald informed us, sell "tiers" branded with our twelve-dollar cocktail infusions. Sheer genius. Missy rolled her eyes so far up in her head I thought she was going to have a stroke.

Despite all the corporate meddling, the hotel was doing decent business and the lounge stayed busy, and like every downtown venue we had our share of "stars" who kept us on our toes. One evening some poor last-year's-model actor in a movie no one had ever heard of ordered up room service and then nearly went into anaphylactic shock because there was shrimp stock in the dish of littleneck clams with applewood bacon lardons. Talk about a scene. I mean twelve people probably saw this guy's "film" and in the end he wasn't even that ill. Call me unsympathetic, but some of these Hollywood types needed a level of L.A. pampering that just wasn't second nature here. Someone in VIP Guest Relations could handle it.

Meanwhile, my recalcitrant sous chef Missy was becoming disgruntled and ending up in hot water over and over again for infractions, both imagined and real. Her zealous perfectionism combined with a fiery temper was a source of constant entertainment to Emily and me, and sheer terror to everyone else in the kitchen. Unfortunately, as executive chef, I was starting to hear about it from above.

This was the pattern—the HR agenda—and it would take precedence over the food repeatedly. Human Resources decided to have a sexual harassment training class at the same time we were supposed to be doing a banquet for eighty advertising executives. Next thing you know, we have eight cooks doodling on the hotel stationery in a meeting room fighting to keep their eyes open while Missy and I are preparing the whole meal—and *still* getting reamed about costs while our kitchen staff learns how to keep their hands off each other, which, trust me, was the least of our problems. Welcome to Hotel Management 101.

Still, I settled in. It wasn't such a bad life going downtown every day, and I was happy to be drawing a decent steady paycheck. My in-laws were living in Seattle and planning a vacation in Juneau, Alaska, of all places. They had managed to convert a working tugboat into their dreamboat yacht—and it had room for us. The forecast for Fourth of July weekend in New York was three days of glorious, 90-degree sunshine beach weather, and we were off on a ten-hour flight to Juneau where the high might reach fifty degrees. Suffice it to say I was less than enthusiastic. I am a devout city guy with a recessive tolerance gene for the country, namely, the country out on the eastern shore of Long Island. Eight days on a converted tugboat seemed a real stretch for me, but with a Dopp kit of prescription meds and antinausea paraphernalia (wristbands, patches, and a hypnosis CD), we headed north by northwest. I did it for love and marriage.

Our seafaring expedition turned out to be nothing short of spectacular. Amy's dad and stepmom are good decent folks and they had done an extraordinary job restoring the boat. The only relatives of mine who did that kind of work probably came over on the *Santa Maria*. Once the meds kicked in, I found myself enthralled by the majesty of the Gulf of Alaska. We had seven days of no land. We saw bears and eagles and caught sockeye salmon, which I sliced open and prepared with a little soy sauce and seawater. We listened to country music nonstop, which would have caused my demise if I hadn't brought along a stash of Chet Baker CDs. There's something otherworldly about Chet Baker singing

"My Funny Valentine" while you're at sea level cruising past a glacier the size of the Chrysler Building. The shifting ice resounded like thunder and the sun barely set even at midnight. We had one bath all week—and that was in a sulphurous hot spring on an island in the middle of nowhere. It was a sensational trip and for all my whining, I was thankful to Amy for dragging me along.

I returned to New York and the chaos of the opening of the Grand's sister hotel. The posh press was all over it and the groovy people came in droves to check it out, which initially cannibalized our business. This in turn made management nervous as hell and put them on the defensive. Vice presidents went on the warpath to cut food costs, cut labor costs, cut everything but electricity for the elevator banks. What's more, the chef at our preening sister hotel had embraced the "tiers" concept more readily than my staff ever had—and the talented fucker was doing it better than I was.

Their profits were cruising along, which put my staff under even more pressure. All of a sudden I was managing a team of deeply unhappy people. It was not a pleasant situation, and I found myself dawdling more and more at home and at the gym before heading downtown to work every day. One morning I was lingering over a cappuccino I had made in the $700 over-the-top espresso machine we received as a wedding gift, when I looked up at the TV and noticed that whatever it was I had been watching had been replaced by a peculiar shot of the World Trade Center, with smoke pouring out of one tower.

I watched in shock until the second plane hit, and then I realized I could no longer just sit there. I needed to get downtown, go to work, do something. I walked out of my building and there was fear and confusion on everyone's faces. No one even knew if the subway was running, and when the train came, I wondered, is this going to blow up, too? We all wondered.

There was an eerie, surreal feeling on the way downtown. Kids were excused from school and on their way home, mostly clueless. Their playful laughter was disturbing and out of place and yet at the same time comforting. The subway car was quiet and then suddenly loud, the voices reaching a crescendo—and then it would go silent just like that. No one knew what the hell was going on. Everyone seemed to be looking at everyone else for solace, for reassurance, for an explanation.

I rode the number 1 local down to Canal Street as I had every day for the last two years. I walked up the stairs out of the subway and looked up, and to my absolute disbelief, where those two enormous towers both stood, was nothing—just puffy clouds and blue sky and billowing black acrid smoke. Part of the city had been amputated. I stood and stared, completely disoriented, and nauseous. There was an awful stench and that cloud of dust and black smoke rising up, and people were walking and running and limping uptown in a trance. I found my way to the hotel and the kitchen was in bedlam. Food was boiling over on the stoves. People were late for work or had not shown up at all. Staff members were yelling. It was utter pandemonium. I screamed at the top of my lungs, *"STOP!* Everybody just stop!" The kitchen went quiet.

We roped it in and started getting our room-service orders out and assessing the situation, since nothing was moving in Manhattan any longer. I went out to the lobby. People were filing in, covered in dust and ash and blood. There were EMS workers, office workers, laborers, hot-dog guys, construction workers. The exodus was north and we were one of the first stops, less than a quarter mile from where the towers had stood. We were ground zero before that word had any meaning in lower Manhattan.

I didn't leave the hotel that night. Amy and I talked several times by phone, separated by the circumstances like so many others who had been affected by the tragedy. The first refugees from Battery Park City and Tribeca were filling the hotel and we were accommodating as many as we could. When I came down the next morning our usually gleaming, polished fancy lounge area was filled with baby strollers and GI Joes, Hot Wheels and Barbies—and moms and dads trying to figure out what to do with their kids who were hungry and scared and exhausted. We had become an impromptu shelter to Tribeca's well-to-do displaced.

In the kitchen we threw out our menu and started preparing pancakes, oatmeal, PB and J's, and cinnamon toast. We put out all of our breakfast cereals and gallons of milk for self-serve. Later in the morning, when the first responders started showing up, we made them enormous omelets and rashers of bacon and toast. We fed them from their all-night rescue effort and then packed them off back to the site with sacks of sandwiches.

That afternoon a chubby cop with a warm expression from the K-9 unit traipsed straight into the kitchen. Did we have anything to feed the dogs that were out on the pile sniffing for bodies? "Dogs?" I asked incredulously. I had the cooks clean out the meat lockers. We sent those hardworking little beasts pounds of filet mignon, lamb, veal, and chicken. I watched the cops drive away in an auxiliary police car with all that meat and I sat down heavily against the service-entrance door. It was the first time I'd seen the outdoors in eighteen hours. I looked up at the eerie orange light coming from the site, trying to come to terms with what had happened. All I could see was this giant phosphorous hole in the sky. I sat there outside the building, leaned up against the rough, cold brick, and cried.

In the weeks to come, we fed cops, firefighters, electricians, medics, you name it, from New York and New Jersey and Washington and California and Pennsylvania. The hotel business was all but gone, dried up, but that was beside the point. I'd never considered myself patriotic, but the sight of six beefy Oklahoma firefighters chowing down on enormous heaping plates of food—they had asked me to make them some "real food"—affected me in a way that no other experience had.

I'm walking along through life getting an education, dating, getting married, getting unmarried, paying my bills, and then literally BOOM, my senses went from unfocused to focused. My life's lens had become a little sharper. I had the ability to cry harder and laugh more heartily. I stopped wasting time, mine and everyone else's. We had taken a hit in New York, and the people we'd once thought ourselves so culturally superior to showed up in droves to bail us out. Even for a cynical bastard like me, I had a newfound sense of pride and patriotism. At the Grand, nobody was worried about flex time or hours or HR issues or who turned up in the penthouse. The owners were committed to the city and to our staff and they were absolutely fair, while looking down the barrel of a very uncertain future for the hotel business in New York.

# Mac & Jeez!

 I'm sitting on the stoop of the brownstone next door to The Waverly, enjoying a late-day espresso before I go in. This is my ritual prior to the predinner meeting with the waitstaff, when I go through the evening's specials. The place, without fanfare or publicity, has gone through the roof. We still have no phone, so there's no way to make a reservation other than access to the e-mail address only the restaurant's closest allies are privy to. The menus still say "Preview" in bold red lettering. Despite the fact we have been open for three months, technically, we are not. I think we had all grown comfortable with this arrangement. If you're not open, you can't screw up. Or at least be judged as harshly as the food media predators would enjoy. Our invisible status, along with the fact that we were jammed to the gills every night, made for a rollicking good time for all.

I have to admit I was relishing this. I had somehow become a part of something very special that was elusive to most everyone else. In my days as a corporate chef, cool was often purchased with cash on the barrelhead. If you could wield it, you had it. At The Waverly, it was a whole different scene. People would ask me for reservations for their friends and they'd justify it by saying, "Oh, he's got money, he'll be your best customer." But it was not about money. It was more about what the Waverly insiders had accomplished. The "big swinging dicks" from Wall Street whom Tom Wolfe had immortalized in *The Bonfire of the Vanities* were not really welcome here. Generally, they were seen as crass, and when we did get a table of them, they would order an expensive bottle of wine and high-five each other every ten minutes. We tended to look more highly on the creative types, like the designer Tom Ford, who was not only immensely successful in business, but magnificently stylish and elegant in his manner. Al Di Meola, the guitarist I idolized in high school, came to the restaurant. This is a guy who played with Return to Forever, Chick Corea's 1970s jazz fusion supergroup. Al is known for his blistering speed and virtuoso technique and has played with the world's most prolific musicians. Of course no one recognized him except me. I shook his hand and asked about a million questions, breaking my own rules about schmoozing with guests. He told me about how he dropped out of Berklee College of Music at nineteen years old and played his first gig as a professional musician at Carnegie Hall. For me this was like meeting Phil Rizzuto. Al likes his steak medium rare. But don't tell the press.

Shortly after we opened, we expanded and took over the apartment above the restaurant. We used it to make room for more vintage wines and, conveniently, to serve as our makeshift office and changing room. I was already in my uniform, chef's jacket and jeans, enjoying the end of a sunny afternoon—my battery-charging time before the shit hits the fan—when a shady-looking guy comes down the completely empty street, stopping at the bottom of the stoop. "You-ah the-chef-ah-here," he asked in an accent that sounded just like my grandfather's, and I immediately recognized it as southern Italian. He gestured toward the restaurant. Our celebrity reputation had become so overblown, I nearly hesitated. Between the food press and reviewers and bloggers and a media starved for access, I was very spare and blatantly apprehensive about who I dished so much as a morsel of information to.

"Maybe," I said hesitantly. "Can I help you?" I asked, thinking he might be a waiter looking for a gig. He came up a step on the stoop and unzipped a frayed, dirty backpack. Was I about to get shot because our hostess had turned some B-list actor away at the door? It was New York, after all. He reached into the bag and a strong earthy smell hit me. I knew instantly what was coming next.

"Tartuffi bianco," he announced, slowly, methodically removing a wrinkled brown lunch bag, the kind my mother used to pack my sandwiches in on my way to grade school. He opened it for me as if he'd just walked out of *The French Connection*. Only it was not heroin he was offering, but white truffles from Alba, fresh off the plane from Italy.

"You like-ah?" he said, handing me the bag full of heavy, dark knotty knobs. I didn't need to sniff it. The funky earthy scent was clear—this was the real deal—the stuff every cheap chemically manufactured truffle oil maker tried to imitate. These nutty little roots were going for around $2,500 a pound. Cash only. The guy's backpack looked heavy. I bet he was carrying close to $40,000 worth of tuber contraband. I asked him where he got them. He smiled a mischievous smile and said nothing. I wondered if he'd held up a produce truck on the Belt Parkway on its way in from Kennedy.

"Pass," I said.

"You ah-sure, maestro? I can-a do maybe-ah little bet-tah for you." He pulled out a small scale from his lumpy backpack, ready to do business.

Odd as this street-corner transaction may seem, it was not totally off the map. I had guys coming to the restaurant all the time trying to hawk their goods. Yesterday, I had a food broker bring in a legitimate cowboy who had hauled ass all the way from a ranch in Montana. The guy wore Wranglers, a four-inch belt buckle, shit-stained boots, and a beat-up Stetson. He had flown to New York with a cooler that had seen better times. It was full of dry ice and thick juicy steaks from his own cattle, from his own ranch. He was trying to cut some big volume business in the Big Apple. And for good reason. If you have a decent product and a top-drawer restaurant makes you their specialty purveyor, it can be worth a fortune in sales and publicity. Just ask the pork guys from Nieman Ranch. We had a local vintner from Long Island who wanted us to carry his wines so badly, he chartered a helicopter to take us out to his vineyard. The chopper picked us up on a windy Saturday morning at the Eastside Heliport and dashed off to the East End in forty-five short minutes, barely enough time for the Xanax to kick in, flying at about a thousand feet with a bird's-eye view of Long Island's gorgeous topography. We landed smack in the middle of the vineyard and walked from the helicopter to the tasting room, where a delicious lunch of Italian *salumi* and antipasti was waiting with tastings of about thirty wines. After coffee and espresso we got back on the chopper and an hour later we were back at work.

"No thanks," I told Truffle Guy. This was a little too shady even for me. But as I walked into The Waverly to start my evening, I had truffles on the brain. Our menu had taken off mainly because of its simplicity and timing—New Yorkers were hankering for a nostalgic take on American dishes from a more innocent time. Nothing too fancy or "chefy" as the partners liked to say. Truffles are fancy, opulent, and downright luxurious by anyone's standards. They were statement food and I didn't see a place for that statement on our menu. But what if I could do something more down-home with truffles? Our biscuits were written about in glossy magazines, and people were clamoring for them. I even made a tray for Helena Christensen, the supermodel, who was having a dinner party at her West Village town house and simply had to have some. She was so desperate that she promised to cook me dinner in return. I delivered the goods but I am still waiting for the dinner invite. Could I devise something that was, like our biscuits, comfort food, jacked up with a bit of the truffle mystique.

The next day I dug out several boxes of Barilla pasta. I decided to go with the cavatappi noodle because I liked the shape and it also happened to be the only pasta we had in dry storage. While the water boiled, I whipped up a light béchamel sauce with milk, flour, and butter, using just enough of the roux to thicken it but not too much, lest it become gummy. I didn't want a heavy, gut-busting plate. I was looking for something small but impactful. When the pasta was cooked al dente I dumped the load into a mixing bowl, adding a healthy dose of an artisan cheddar, parmagiano Reggiano, and a few other ingredients I liked to keep up my sleeve. I transferred the whole concoction into a hotel pan and baked it at 400 degrees in the convection oven until the dish was bubbling and the top had browned just crunchy and right. I called Emil in and scooped a little out onto a plate for each of us. I grabbed a small knob of truffle that I had purchased on the way to work, along with a stainless-steel truffle slicer that I had scored at a local Village gourmet shop. I sliced several healthy paper-thin rounds of truffle on top of the steaming macaroni and cheese. I sampled it first. Then I handed the plate to Emil. He took a forkful, warily. "So?" I asked.

"Not bad," he said, characteristically. From Emil that was as good as a James Beard Award. The next evening we put Macaroni & Cheese with Shaved White Truffle on the specials menu at $55 a serving. For better or worse, our signature dish was born.

My haphazard culinary hybrid took on a life of its own. What I had intended as a fun dish to occasionally spruce up the daily specials became larger than life. People couldn't get enough of the stuff. I had to start stocking the ultra-expensive fungus, at enormous cost. The ceremony of shaving those tasty little morsels of white truffle often fell on me, which meant I found myself running out of the kitchen two dozen times a night to mingle with my truffle-struck guests, which struck me as rather odd. One night I did my truffle-shaving dance for a shapely, very young and insanely sexy woman who was at the Waverly no doubt on Daddy's black Amex. When I was done slicing the three curls of truffle on her bowl of steaming noodles she stood up and kissed me so hard on the lips that I nearly landed in the lap of the woman at the table behind me. I had never considered the aphrodisiacal qualities of the truffle. It seemed the oyster, lowly bivalve that it was, had new-found competition.

While fifty-five bucks for a plate of macaroni and cheese (give or take a hundred for market fluctuations) might seem extreme to the stroller set, in fact we were offering up a superb value. You could have your spaghetti with butter and truffles for north of a hundred dollars at any of a dozen places in the Village alone, and no one batted an eyelash. But our cozy, popular plate of Mac & Cheese had the press up in arms. *Entertainment Tonight* camped outside on Bank Street poking a microphone into the noses of our neighbors. "Tell us, sir, what do you think of paying fifty-five dollars for a plate of macaroni and cheese?" The *New York Times* did its usual, stately mocking of the new kid on the block's audacious offering. My cell phone number got leaked, and I found myself deleting furious messages, as if I had just poisoned the city's water supply. A food writer from the *Daily News* got a hold of me and asked for a reservation. We had a strict policy at The Waverly—everyone, including reviewers, paid their own tab. Mr. Food Journalist and his guest sat at the bar and each ordered up the Mac & Cheese in question. I noticed, even as the company credit card hit the table, that they had both cleaned their plates. This seemed a good sign.

The next day, as I'm reading along with three million of my fellow man-on-the-street New Yorkers, I open the review page to a three-inch blaring headline: MAC & *JEEZ!* I was cooked again. The media loved to hate us or perhaps hated to love us. For weeks you could not open the *Post, Daily News,* or *Times* and not read about our "overpriced" pasta. There was little I could do but grin and bear it and watch as we sold over thirty orders of the stuff a night, while the media howled in protest along the sidelines.

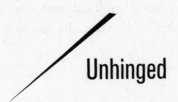

# Unhinged

Exceeding anyone's expectations of what was to be during those first months after 9/11, New York City began to get back on its feet. There was a can-do attitude reflected especially by the people downtown who had lost so much. The city created opportunities to get businesses re-opened as soon as possible. The Tribeca Film Festival was created to draw New Yorkers and the outside world back downtown. And at the hotels, we were back, too. Occupancy increased, new staff was hired, and much to my surprise, I was made corporate chef of the whole enter-prise. It was unexpected because the other chef seemed so much more of a company man.

Of course my bump in prestige did nothing to change the ongo-ing love affair between me and Human Resources. In fact they were all over me worse than ever for every transgression imaginable. I was even reprimanded for "dressing inappropriately in public space." Apparently jeans and a chef coat suddenly violated some corporate code of fashion ethics. Add to the mix my thick unruly hairstyle and face stubble, and I had become the notorious poster boy for what new hires should not do. There was no doubt I was wearing my welcome thin.

Soon after I was named top gun, I was trying to lay down the law with a cook named Juan, a persnickety young cooking school graduate who liked to start sentences with the words "Chef, I think . . ." The menu at that point featured a dish of braised short beef ribs garnished with diced root vegetables finished with a braising liquid. Not a culinary tour de force, but executed properly, a good solid dish nonetheless. The celery, carrots, and parsnips had to be diced in precise quarter-inch cubes. The recipe uses about a half-cup of the vegetables per order, along with minced shallots and a little garlic sautéed in olive oil. The vegetables hit the blazing sauté pan just a moment before serving and there you have it. This was not brain surgery. A little skill and a lot of heart, and most anyone can do it.

At seven p.m., when we should have been up and running at full speed, there was Juan whiling away his time with a cutting board full of vegetables in their natural raw state not nearly ready for dinner service. "Juan, what are you doing?" I inquired impatiently.

He stared at me like I had just asked to sleep with his girlfriend. "I'm chopping celery, Chef."

"*Now* you're chopping celery?"

"Yes, Chef."

"What the hell have you been doing for the last two hours?"

"Well, I was grating nuts for the pecan pancakes for the brunch menu."

"Really? Sunday brunch? Why not start on the menu for the fucking Tuesday banquet while you're at it?" Up to that point I'd been doing a pretty good job of controlling my temper. We were a nonunion house and there was no offending the staff, lest they vote to unionize, which would cost the hotel untold dollars. Management liked to remind us of that about every half hour.

Juan took the hint and started dicing, all the while explaining why he was not doing the thing that he was supposed to be doing two hours ago and all of the good reasons why he *was* doing it now at the height of the dinner crush.

"Chef, I think—" he starts.

"Juan, shut the fuck up," I said finally, interrupting him. OK, now my patience was wearing thin. Talk about a kitchen going silent. The only sound you could hear was the *chop chop chop* of Juan's knife as he stared down at his shoes, not to mention the unspoken gratitude of every other cook who had to listen to this bullshit for thirty-five hours a week with two ten-minute breaks daily. If Juan knew the recipes as well as he knew the company benefits package, then we'd have something.

The next day, via a very well written e-mail, I found myself summoned to the office of Human Resources, yet again. The latest hire on this floor where I spent so much time was named Tiffany. She was attractive in an eighties sort of way: navy suit, Ann Taylor blouse, one button too many undone, shiny black mile-high pumps, skirt well above where it needed to be, and an uncharacteristic fake tan. I sat down in her office, fish blood streaking my apron, shoes covered in chicken fat, soaking up space in an expensive office chair.

"So, Chef?" she asked. I wasn't too sure how much power she had, but the tone of her voice suggested that I at least pay her lip service. Her appearance confounded me. I really was trying to pay attention until my eye wandered to those pumps and I noticed, at the side of her desk, a striped, pink shopping bag from a very familiar lingerie retailer. Was the new HR veepee thong material? I tried to concentrate.

"I've had some complaints registered in your employee file," Tiffany announced, bringing me crashing back down to earth.

My thoughts went immediately to the food. I had no clue what she was talking about. Was my waitstaff betraying me? I was the first and only person who needed to know if any dishes were being sent back from the dining room uneaten. Anything less would be mutiny.

"One of your cooks talked to the steward about your *management style*," she continued.

"Management style?" I asked. I didn't even know I had a style. There were no drug busts in my file. No slipping out for AA meetings. No plate- or knife-throwing incidents. By restaurant chef standards, I was a pussy.

"Ohhh," I said. "Juan. Yes, he's annoying as hell to everyone in the kitchen and he wasn't prepared for work on time. I told him if he didn't have his celery ready, I'd have him on the next boat back to the mother country. Problem?"

The silence settled over Tiffany's office like a fallen soufflé. She smiled at me coldly, but at least it was still a smile.

"Have you ever considered controlling your temper, John?"

"You're kidding," I said. Her expression suggested otherwise. I reassessed and decided getting in any deeper with HR over this minor infraction was hardly worth it. I flashed her the best smile I could muster and said, "No worries, I'll take care of it. Anything else you need?" There was a long pause. It was a loaded question and I sensed her intrigue. I jumped out of my chair and got out of there before I could get into any more trouble. I scheduled Juan for nights, weekends, and every holiday on the calendar until his suspect fastidiousness began to subside. I inconvenienced him into submission. Mission accomplished.

Life, unfortunately, had not grown troublesome just at the office. As much as I hated to admit it, after five years of dating and almost the same amount married, Amy and I were drifting apart, and drifting was something I knew way too much about. I desperately did not want a repeat performance of my last marital meltdown. Amy had grown weary of the retail clerk existence, and she and a friend had started a small mail-order business. It had not exactly leapt into the black, so she had also started tending bar again. I had been so busy holding down the kitchens of two hotels that I barely knew what she was doing, but I had a strong sense that I should be concerned—for both of us. I decided we needed a night on the town to see if we couldn't reignite the fire that had once blazed in the country and now was barely smoldering. Superchef Jean-Georges Vongerichten had recently opened his contemporary take on a Chinese restaurant, complete with a shark tank in the main dining room and a three-week waiting list. I made a call and landed us a good table.

Amy, as usual, looked like a million bucks, and based on that alone, it was hard not to fall in love with her all over again. Still, the distance between us was unmistakable as we lingered over tropical cocktails and fried crab and lotus seed, garlicky frogs legs, and steamed lobster in ginger. Lost in the chattering buzz of the austere, high-style dining room was any remote sense of connection. The number of ballooning silences was alarming and nothing I said seemed to close the gap. It was way too reminiscent of a place I had been before. When I casually made an innocent quip about our newlywed friends whose wedding we had recently attended, Amy burst into sobs over her e-fu noodles. It was not a good sign. Even our inscrutable waitress in her Vivian Tam–designed uniform was taken aback by the loud, distressing sobs.

A few weeks later we were watching an episode of *Seinfeld* on the orange puffy couch. We gazed at the TV, locked in stony silence in our own private spaces, nothing wrong and yet nothing especially right. Finally, I looked over at her and said, "We don't have a whole lot left to say to each other, do we?" She nodded, as a tear ran down her cheek and made the tiniest salty splash on my forearm. It might have been the saddest and most amicable end to a marriage ever.

# Adrenaline Junkie

I moved downtown to a small Greenwich Village studio I had purchased with an inheritance from a late aunt. She would have been pleased if she knew the tiny fortune she had left me would help me get back on my feet and, consequently, put me at last back in the middle of exactly where I wanted to be. Meanwhile, the general manager at the Grand was about to jump ship to a new hotel on the border of New York's Chelsea neighborhood. After he had cut his deal, he let me know that the owners were preparing to open an epic Italian restaurant on the ground-floor plaza, taking up an entire city block. This had a very good ring to it.

The Maritime Hotel was a converted, portholed edifice that once housed the National Maritime Union of America and then later a home for wayward kids. The hotel was planted squarely on the northeast border of what is known as the Meatpacking District, where meat had been processed since 1890. In its heyday, whole carcasses would line the streets, hanging from thick steel hooks as the packers would carve them up, filling custom orders for restaurants near and far. Experienced, lifelong butchers would cut steaks and chops, veal and lamb with the precision of a surgeon and the flair of an artist. Their craft ensured just the right amount of protein-to-fat ratio, impossible to accomplish by machine, which makes all the difference in a porterhouse steak, for example. Escalating rents and higher wages for skilled labor created a changing business climate, however, and not for the better. More efficient machines in larger plants took over the bulk of the work, cutting out the meatpacker altogether, marking the end of yet another industrial neighborhood in New York.

This formerly deserted portion of town, mostly known for funky all-night diners, transsexual hookers, and gigantic well-fed rats, was poised for lift-off because of large, now-available retail spaces. Since no one had really lived there in the past, there were very few complaints about drunk patrons or noisy garbage trucks at four a.m. That meant far less hassle for restaurant or nightclub owners to get their licenses and operate.

I'd been at the Grand nearly four years, longer than I'd been at any job. I was on a fast track to nowhere, managing uninspired employees getting fat on inflated guaranteed wages and job security—and I was dangerously close to becoming one of them. I was answering, or more accurately, not answering to corporate more than I was creating anything unique in the kitchen, or even cooking, for that matter. It seemed as good a time as any to consider a change.

I interviewed with one of the principal partners of the new hotel and restaurant space, a guy named Sean who had scored terrific success on both coasts with the most happening food-and-drink establishments. He was well ensconced in the world of art, film, music, and fashion and had been a West Coast insider for many years. I had a gut sense he would be a good guy to align myself with.

The Maritime Hotel filled 9th Avenue between 16th and 17th Streets. Set above the avenue was the lobby of the hotel and the outdoor plaza that was to become the property's latest addition, La Bottega. The Maritime already housed a nightclub and a new, popular, and stunning Japanese restaurant that was drawing in throngs of all the right people every night. One look at the space for La Bottega and my palms got sweaty.

The kitchen was set up like a gigantic horseshoe, with a monstrous pass for the outgoing plates—two stainless-steel shelves, twenty-four inches wide, complete with heat lamps so that the food would stay warm for its mile-long journey to the tables. It could feed a thousand, and it would have to. The hot line alone had three heavy-duty six-burner ranges, two fryers, a thirty-six-inch grill and double stack convection oven, along with an enormous steam kettle and French braiser for making the copious amounts of stock that would be necessary for gallons of soup and sauces. On the opposite wall was an equally impressive cold line for salads, antipasti, and a dessert staging area. A two-thousand-pound wood-burning pizza oven was installed with a six-foot stone hearth transported from Washington State. The restaurant reflected the sensibility of its owners, laid back and relaxed with lots of natural wood and a soulful feel. There were hundreds of pounds of prosciutti and salumi hanging on antique cast-iron meat hooks on the wall adjacent to the pizza oven. Basically, it was a dream space, only larger. When Sean made me an offer to become the executive chef, I took my time to think about it. I had made so many rash decisions in the past. It was a huge job and I already had a huge job. I really liked that pizza oven, though. I accepted the offer.

We were dedicated to bringing in the best people to La Bottega—a great sous chef, a pastry person, and a truly inspired pizza maker and consultant who was our Italian in charge of all things Italian. Marco helped us source the finest burrata from Italy with a delectable creamy center that he told us only he could get because the supplier would *only* sell to Italians. This was complete bullshit, of course, the kind of crap you'd see written on a cheesy Italian menu, but Marco was such an eccentric guy, you could put up with it just to get that cheese. It was fun to behold him testing olive oils and dough recipes. We made at least ten varieties, and I sampled pizza in all five boroughs of the city to compare to our handiwork and make sure ours stood out, cooking up pie after pie in the wood-burning oven until it was just right. Meanwhile, I was developing pasta dishes and a wide range of seafood—carpaccio di pulpo, tonno con fave, and salmone con carciofi. We created a Greatest Hits list of Italian desserts that included tiramisu, cannoli, cheesecakes made with mascarpone and ricotta, and affogato, which is simply gelato floating in freshly brewed espresso. We did all of this with an eye toward executing at least fifty or more portions of each per night. That staggering number alone would change the whole perspective of the menu development process.

We finally opened around Halloween of 2002 to a mob scene. The place was crammed to the rafters and the pizza oven was going full tilt and the place had the aroma of a cozy smoky fire like something good was cooking and the people kept coming and coming. The buzz was approaching fever pitch and it was obvious that we had a bona fide hit on our hands. We employed upwards of forty staff members working twelve hours a day for sixty straight days, all with one single-minded goal—to run the best possible restaurant we could. It was a complete bummer to read the disparaging *New York Times* review that came out only a few Wednesdays after we opened, but it did nothing to slow the masses. It did, however, dispirit the staff, and it took several weeks for those of us closest to the project to go through the five stages of grief. When I finally reached acceptance, I boycotted the *Times* for a month. The owners, on the other hand, were focused on receipts. The only review that mattered to them was in the nightly bottom line, and that write-up was glowing.

Everything I had done up to this point in my career was dwarfed by the sheer immensity of the place. If I paused for more than a minute to think about it, I'm sure I would have freaked. Fortunately, I never found that minute.

"Felipe, I need twenty steaks total on the grill, now!" It was Thursday night and we were jammed to the gills, and the orders were spitting out of the kitchen food printer, spewing curls into great scrolled loops on the floor. I looked over and realized there must be tickets for at least ten tables down there I hadn't even seen yet. "Diego, how many chickens you got, baby?" I screamed. "We got twenty tables waiting for food."

Holy shit, I thought, if Matt hasn't covered my ass, it's over. I mean I am toast. Running out of chickens at 9:30 is not cool. People do not want to wait an hour for a table only to be told, "Sorry, out of that." I called Matt at home, waking his ass up and asked how many chickens he ordered?

"Thirty-five. Short today boss," he said sleepily. "Sorry."

*"Thirty-five?"* I shouted into the phone loud enough to wake his neighbors. "That doesn't get us to ten o'clock, dude. We're not short on customers. Get me some chicken, *now,* amigo!"

Matt was my executive steward, the guy in charge of all the food purchasing—a key position in a high-volume restaurant like ours. He was a big white mountain of a man with an inexplicable Asian last name and a bunch of artfully done tattoos on his visible extremities. He was a guy you probably didn't want to see in a Speedo. He had a head for numbers and portion control, in particular, feeding customers in a cost-effective, waste-free manner. We were good for one hundred branzini, two hundred dry-aged sirloin steaks, fifteen cases of fresh spinach, ten cases of beefsteak tomatoes, and about sixty-five chickens on a Thursday night—a night when, last I peeked, the young and curious downtown habitués were lined up three-deep at the bar. This was nuts, considering we had nearly three hundred seats.

Sweat was running down my back. Eighteen burners, 30,000 BTU of firepower each, were blasting away while I manned the expediting station, moving out food like air traffic control at LaGuardia on Memorial Day weekend. I had three rare steaks in the window under the heat lamps waiting for tomato salads to accompany them. They wouldn't be rare for long. Those infrared heat lamps could bring soup to a boil if you kept it there long enough. "Guys, stop what you're doing right now and give me three fucking tomato salads, now. Thank you, amores," I call out, thinking, Please, dear God, where are my goddamned chickens?

Twenty minutes later and just in the nick of time, a five-foot-two Latin dude whom I've never laid eyes on in my life shows up with two dozen birds in two plain brown shopping bags, which Felipe can now butcher on the fly. Turns out the guy with the chickens used to work with Matt at the last place he worked and owed him a favor. Nice work, Matty, I thought.

At that moment Mindy, a knockout black waitress with a curly mane of hair whose uniform was far too short for her svelte five-foot-eleven frame, stuck her head through the transom, all business. "Chef, some lady on 26 wants to know if the mushrooms are wild or cultivated?" I looked up from the grill burner that was flaring so hot it nearly seared my eyebrows from five feet away. Eight New York strip steaks flew off and hit the plates, beautifully charred and steaming hot. Four line cooks all helped add the patate alla nonna onto the plates, and then the Swiss chard braised in a little wine, a brush of unfiltered extra virgin oil on each. Go!

"Chef?" Mindy implored. It wasn't like she didn't have her hands full, with two eight-tops, a deuce, and a table of six investment bankers, wasted drunk, trying for the last half hour to get her to bend over.

"Tell her they were hand-picked by a bigamist sect on the outskirts of Oregon," I said. For chrissakes, who were these people? Too much time on their hands and too much goddamned Food TV. Matt calls Mushrooms R Us, they come with two hundred boxes from wherever the hell there are mushrooms this time of year and he opens one box. If they look and smell like a dark, rich fungus and a rat doesn't jump out, he signs. I'm all for the locavore movement, and whatever I can get locally, I do. But we're going to do a thousand covers by night's end. If you want fresh wild mushrooms, buy a house someplace damp, go into the woods, and forage away.

The laundry service is putting too much starch in my chef coat and the heat is giving me a rash on my forearm as I help Raoul plate four veal Milanese, one no breading. The printer is spitting out orders like confetti, and eight line cooks are firing on twelve cylinders while I'm plating, calculating, and screaming out orders. Out of the corner of my eye, I see Felipe is digging for more whole branzini lying in a pool of watery fish blood, reminding me that the fridge guy is coming tomorrow to check the thermostats. A little *E. coli* would be really bad for business.

"Pizza Margarita to the bar," I call out. At a bar as busy as ours, the food runners are always confused, so the bartenders type in descriptions on the computer so that the food can find its rightful owner. This dupe reads "SEAT 14 GIGANTIC TITS." I'm no attorney, but there may well be a law against this sort of thing. Still, this is a restaurant, not a city agency, and I intercept the plate. Helping the troops builds morale. Plus I'd overheard one of my best Italian waiters talking about this particular patron the whole night. After all, there is only one thing Italian waiters know better than food. It was the least I could do.

As I walk briskly through the corridor that leads to the dining room I nearly trip over Ramon, one of the countless busboys we employ. He is standing still at a tray station holding a pint glass filled to the rim with fresh-squeezed orange juice. This shit is more expensive than gasoline. I stop and stare, the pizza searing my outstretched hand. "What the fuck are you doing?" I ask. Would he, if he worked in a bank, help himself to a stack of twenties just because it was there?

"*Lo siento, jefe,*" he says. Great. He's sorry. I wonder if he even knows who I am. I walk out to the bar. Not hard to find "gigantic tits." She is surrounded by a grove of towering suits, plying her with sixteen-dollar Cosmos. Why are those guys always so fucking tall? I set down her pizza and hightail it back to the kitchen. In the corridor near the coffee station, I stop in my tracks. Ramon has not moved. He's just finished his glass of fresh-squeezed. In fact, he looks as if he may help himself to another.

There is a moment between us, a pause like the split second between the fuse and the bomb about to detonate in the Road Runner cartoons. Screw up once, no worries. I am still your friend. But dare me on my dime and I am no longer responsible for my actions. I launched into Ramon with a string of invectives that impressed even the non-English-speaking staff. It was not that I objected to his need to hydrate. I could have even turned my head on his quaffing liquid gold this one time. But with endless tables backed up and a kitchen running in full overdrive?

When I was done in English, I resorted to every Spanish obscenity I had learned in all my years of cooking. Ramon and I were eyebrow to eyebrow and Christ knows where it might have gone except that Jason, my evening sous chef and most unlikely voice of reason, mercifully intervened. With the severed heart tattoo gleaming on his neck and a quivering carotid artery bulging beneath it, he brought just the right blend of threat and diplomacy to the potentially lethal situation. Jason chattered off a few sentences in Spanish and Ramon slunk back to his station a little less thirsty.

"What the hell got into you, Chef?" Jason asked.

"I'm fine," I mumbled. At least no cutlery had been brandished. Back at the expediting station I grabbed some more dupes out of the printer and regrouped. No choice but to get back in the game, pronto. "Six chicken, four steaks, four fennel salads, Papi, let's go, let's go, now! Desserts, pick up. Hold it, hold it. This chocolate cake looks like shit. Hold the other three desserts and make me another. Fast. The fucking gelato is melting. C'mon!" Wiping my brow with a soaked hand towel I looked at my watch. We still had two hours to go.

Then, out of the chaos a sweet scent found it's way up my nostrils, obscuring all others in the kitchen. Christina! She had saucer-like brown eyes and auburn hair that fell adorably out of her tight ponytail, a dancer's body sculpted and visible somehow beneath her boyishly nautical waitress uniform. I had promised myself no more getting involved with girls at the restaurant. But Christina, a struggling songwriter, had invited me to her East Village apartment and played me her audition tape one night after closing—that mellow, awful, droning acoustic chick rock. Instead of following my first instinct and jumping out her first-floor window, I listened and told her how talented she was. Good move. Those eyes, that face, that body. My resolve wilted like baby spinach. The reward was blissful.

She walked by with a loaded tray: two affogato, an apple crostada, and two ricotta cheesecakes with strawberries macerated with thyme. I silently prayed that my prep guy didn't kill the cheesecakes when he yanked them for 150 pounds of veal bones he needed to roast for stock. I felt a tap on my ankle. Somehow, even with a loaded tray, Christina had surreptitiously issued me a summons with her navy blue nautical Keds. How could legs look so good in such goofy shoes? I smiled at her as she glided by. Half of the staff will wrap it up tonight with a fat joint, or maybe a few lines at the club down the block notorious for its sexually ambiguous cocktail servers, not to mention their very lenient policy on recreational drug usage. Not me. One whiff of that Coco Chanel on her neck and I knew where I was headed.

Finally, we come up for air. It's close to one a.m. and breakfast service at The Maritime starts in five hours. Hopefully there are enough organic eggs for the LAX–JFK redeye flight chockful of actors, agents, and coke fiends who'll be blazing in at dawn looking for their protein fix. Would Angel, my overnight chef, even show up for his shift? I could call over to his favorite watering hole and check how the tequila consumption was going. It was usually a good barometer. Mostly he showed. Ask more and you're setting your expectations way too high.

The night was slowing down. We'd done nearly a thousand dinners. I hadn't found time to trade notes with Matt. I'm thinking twenty-five pounds of tuna, six whole salmon, and a whole lot of New York strip steaks. Christ knows how many chickens with Friday night coming. I still had to check how badly my cooks had trashed the vegetable walk-in refrigerator in their rush to leave the building and get their beer on.

The scent of Christina lingered. I felt a new burst of adrenaline kicking in. Did the job find me or I was just hard-wired for this kind of existence? Shouldn't I be settled by now? A couple of kids maybe? Some real adult responsibility? There's that Coco Chanel again, the scent pulling me in as if taunting me through the kitchen exhaust system. We kicked ass tonight. I fed a lot of people. Happy people. The night was young. New York would sleep well. I would, too. Much later.

# Coda

At some point along the way I suppose I came of age in the restaurant business. In more ways than I bargained for. They say there are no second acts, but I was well into the meaty part of mine.

The time I spent at La Bottega represented the best and worst of everything I aspired to when I had this crazy notion that cooking might be a lot more fun than playing a game of darts with the careers of insurance executives. You'd think at this stage I would have been inured to restaurant reviews, but oddly enough, the *Times* review of La Bottega stung more than I expected. I'd had my share of bad reviews, but this was different. It actually unnerved me. I wondered what would happen next. Would I be fired? Would someone have to take the fall? What if people stopped coming? One reviewer's exception with her rigatoni piselli changed my perception of my role as a chef, and when the place took off in spite of her scathing words, that changed my perception even more. Finally, after all these years, I felt like I had permission to do what I do. You just had to look out into the dining room on one of our crazy, packed nights to see that it worked. At so many of my stops along the way I was cooking for any number of reasons—to learn about French techniques, to perfect a veal stock, or make the silkiest gnocchi imaginable. Or just to pay the rent. I'd picked up a lot along the way. But never before now did I feel so responsible for one thing—to send people home well-fed and happy. La Bottega was a customer-driven restaurant, not a chef-driven one. It was a distinction I would learn to be OK with while I was there.

Our business was very much a seasonal affair because of the sprawling outdoor plaza and the many extra seats we had to fill from March until October. We quadrupled our numbers in the warm weather months and that was the good news. However, by the end of the second season the business had leveled off and the owners began to amortize my salary by outsourcing me across other properties in their empire. I was being sent to Los Angeles, and I had also picked up private consulting gigs on my own, which took me to Boston, to Arlington, Virginia, and other markets that were of little interest to me. I found myself creating menus and analyzing staffing and being tasked with reining in costs. I shouldn't have been surprised. I had acquired all of these skills along the way.

I respected the owners a great deal and took on their assignments without complaint. I'd come a long way from feeling like the ground was constantly rushing up at me, but I still needed something that had my fingerprints on it. La Bottega was not that place. Consequently, I was not shocked when Sean called me in one day and informed me that I had basically priced myself out of a job. Like much of the cost-cutting work I had been doing for the owners, the time had come for them to cut La Bottega's costs—and that meant giving me the ax. Specifically, Sean told me that I had done an outstanding job and that we'd do a nice place together, "someday." Businessman that he was, he then proceeded to list all the parameters of what he would consider a "nice place." Small and intimate, yet large enough to do a high sales volume. Perfect location, preferably with an outdoor space component. Fully outfitted kitchen requiring not a drop of work. Low rent. High ceilings. Wide dining room.

Narrow cost margins. And all of this with an ocean view. No one had ever been fired so gracefully and with such promise for the future.

Frankly, I was not especially disappointed. It had been a crazy time at La Bottega, living *la vida loca* in the heart of the Meatpacking District. Almost sixteen years had passed while I toiled in the trenches of the New York City restaurant scene. I'd been through a half-dozen new homes, two marriages, and more friends, women, and relationships than I could count. At last I was starting to get some sense of who I was. With any luck I might be done with therapy in another ten years or so.

For the first time since I had descended the steps into the basement of Dean & DeLuca, I found myself taking time to think about my next move. I had the big-restaurant résumé plus a network of vastly connected chefs, cooks, and restaurant owners to help me land a job quickly. But I didn't want just a job. If I had learned anything through all of this, it was to follow my heart and, finally, listen to and trust my instinct.

New York had changed. The city, the neighborhoods, the people. There was money, loads of it, but then New York had always had a history of money. Maybe what was different was people's tastes. They had sampled fresh and local and good food, and they were becoming health-conscious, quality-conscious, and environmentally conscious. A decent piece of line-caught fish prepared simply with local ingredients was not just a passing trend. I had gone through the rigors of training with some of the best chefs that New York had to offer, and in the end what I came away with was a handful of useful skills and an innate sense of what worked. I'd slaved for geniuses and madmen and learned something from both. I'd been in charge of kitchens so small you couldn't turn around without meeting up with a searing sauté pan or the pointed end of a Wusthof knife poking your ass, as well as kitchens large enough to drive a '74 Cadillac through.

As I lay in bed one late summer's morning, I had a head full of dreams and aspirations and not a place in the world to be. It was still early enough in the day to enjoy the city before the sultry blanket of August settled in like silt. I hauled my three-speed copper-colored Schwinn down in the elevator and meandered slowly off in search of my first espresso. The Village was quiet. Most everyone had decamped to the Hamptons for the last days of summer. I pedaled lazily down Bank Street, no real destination in mind. At the corner of Bank and Waverly Place, I noticed a commercial "For Rent" sign in the window of a lovely building. It couldn't have been there long, I thought. A space and location like this would be gone in a week. Restaurateurs in New York have brokers looking for just this kind of thing full-time. I'd peddled by this corner maybe a thousand times before and never stopped once. I got off my bicycle to explore.

I peered in the window past the "For Rent" sign. The closed up place had once been a restaurant. Daylight barely filtered in, illuminating a heavy wooden bar. The tables were still there, frozen in time. They were probably so busted up and rickety that the previous owner couldn't squeeze a penny out of their resale. I stared in the window, trying to make out the lay of the interior. I locked my bicycle to a street sign and wandered around the corner. Much to my surprise, the shuttered restaurant spread back to a secluded courtyard with a huge oak tree growing straight out of a tarp roof. The garden space was so perfect you could almost hear the clinking of ice and the babble of conversation. It amazed me that I had never set foot in here before. As I gazed in at the remnants of what it had once been, the street could not have been more quiet. I wondered how long the place had been available for rent.

My investor friend Andy lived nearby on one of these tree-lined Village blocks. Maybe he'd know something. He always did. I called him on his cell phone, wondering if he was at the beach. He picked up right away. "Andy, what do you know about a boarded-up restaurant down on Bank Street?" I asked.

"I know the landlord," he replied. "Why?"

Within an hour I was traipsing through the thick dust on the floors as the landlord sized me up. The interior was mostly dark—very dark with low, beamed ceilings and ancient worn banquettes. Still, light filtered in from the bar up front as well as the garden area in the back. Examining the place from the inside, it looked like it could do a hundred seats easy with a new expanded floor plan. I walked through the tiny cramped pass to what remained of the kitchen. It was small but functional. You could craft a pretty good workspace, I thought. I strolled back out to the main floor.

The landlord's handshake was desultory. He must have had twenty-five people call, chomping at the bit. There were precious few spaces like this left in the city. He locked the front door and was gone without fanfare. I sat down on the stoop of the brownstone next door. It was an amazing corner, silently hidden just a half block from the noise and bustle of 7th Avenue South. Sunlight dappled off the enormous shade tree that hung above the street. I took a deep breath and drank my coffee in silence. Then I got out my cell phone and dialed.

"Sean," I said when he picked up. "I found our place." Just a little more than a year later The Waverly served its first customer.

# Epilogue

I'm standing in line at JFK to board a flight to Miami to attend what may well be the largest epicurean gathering ever assembled on the planet—the South Beach Wine & Food Festival. Upwards of 35,000 people have purportedly paid twelve hundred dollars to eat, sample, taste, and quaff at 540 "official" events ranging from a $500-a-head tribute dinner for Jean-Georges Vongerichten, to an obesity awareness event for children given by Arthur Agatston, the author of *The South Beach Diet*. I've been cherry-picked for service at this monster food fest by its organizer, Lee Brian Schrager, who had enjoyed several meals at The Waverly in the past. After fourteen months of wall-to-wall press for our celebrity clientele, it seemed like my tiny star had begun its ascent. All of a sudden, my name is all over the Web, in the paper, and in magazine articles, oftentimes with comments I have no recollection of giving. A food writer of note who a year ago wouldn't have spoken to me is calling for tasty quotes on my cell phone.

The attention is both flattering and a little mortifying. I've been asked to come to South Beach and hang out with the likes of Bobby Flay, Mario

Batali, Florence Tyler, Tony Bourdain, Emeril Lagasse—even Rocco Di-Spirito, rising like a phoenix, is on the guest list. It was daunting, to say the least.

As our line to board the plane creeps forward, I recognize a chef I know who hasn't had his own restaurant in years. Before I can even say hello he recognizes me and gives me a big "Yo, dog, what's up bro'," acting madly cool and relevant. He's wearing some very expensive aviator sunglasses and a thick gold chain. When did he become "street"? I wonder. He cuts past the rest of us and disappears down the jetway. A lady on line asks me, "Who was that?"

"A chef," I say, nonchalantly.

"Oh, I've seen his show. Gosh, I love his food!"

Huhhh? This guy hasn't served a plate of anything to a soul outside of a TV studio in years, and she loves his food? It used to be that chefs—the guys and girls with burned forearms and chronic back pain—were the cornerstone of the restaurant business, the unheralded gatekeepers of the total food experience. In fact, wasn't I one of them? The woman hears our section called and bolts around me like I'm invisible. Guess she hadn't partaken of The Waverly experience. I follow her onto the plane, schlepping my carry-on luggage over my shoulder as I walk down the center of the narrow aisle. I almost knock over Mr. TV Food Personality's complimentary first-class cocktail on my way to my seat in row 34.

The South Beach Food & Wine Festival is spring break for food professionals, replete with all the debauchery normally reserved for those with less adult responsibility. My flight plunks me down in the terminal at Miami International Airport, where I am greeted by a sea of silly sun hats, *turista* fashions, and an abundance of overly cheerful women in pastel colors clashing with bulging men in tube socks and sandals. One gets the sense we'd been diverted to Orlando. Crowds are milling about the information booth and I'm actually starting to feel like I'm in the wrong place. Mister TV Food Guy is nowhere to be seen. Then I see a staff member with a placard with my name on it. That's more like it. I am led to a waiting van and shuffled off to my hotel.

The festival provides lodging for all the many attending chef "personalities," as we are billed on the Web site. This is a new title for my résumé. I had not actually noted where I was staying. I'd been to South Beach plenty of times, and the area where the festival was taking place was full of cool Art Deco hotels. "Retro" was probably a generous description for where the van dropped me and a couple of the other "personalities." I'd say it was aspiring to retro, once they got around to tearing it down. Still, in my room I found a welcome gift bag awaiting me, overflowing with more cooking-related promotional goods than a Williams-Sonoma store. I never knew there were so many paring knives, citrus zesters, microplanes, bottled waters, bottle openers, designer jams, organic nuts, Wisconsin cheeses, Nicaraguan chocolates, and espressos from Italy, Seattle, and a small local roaster in Maine. Additionally, laid out neatly across my bed was one more item—a South Beach Wine & Food Festival chef's jacket, fitted just perfectly for me. The nifty coat had enough sponsor logos to decal an Indy racecar. My spirits picked up sufficiently enough that I decided to leave my spartan hotel room and find the festival's headquarters, where I figured I could get registered and perhaps catch up with a few friends.

I needed only follow the masses down Collins Avenue until I spied a corral of network satellite trucks with their towering antennae poking up into the blue Miami sky like waiting scorpions. Yep, this was the place. I walked into the lobby, where I was greeted by TV crews, camera lights, boom guys, camera guys, all churning about amid a sea of cables and gear. I squeezed past the very buttoned-up NBC team where Matt Lauer was doing a taped interview with someone I could barely make out beyond the throng of women who had gathered to witness the spectacle. A kindly festival intern sensed my bewilderment as I wandered the lobby, and she led me up to Chef Registration on the third floor, where a table was set up with every snack, beverage, and sweet imaginable. I was handed yet another bag full of goodies and a very impressive laminated purple badge. Even the lanyard I placed around my neck had sold out its ad space to a pasta sponsor. This was big business.

I'd been invited to this extravaganza to participate in "Best of the Best." About two dozen of my fellow chefs from around the country and I were tasked with preparing a signature dish from our restaurants. Rumor had it over a thousand people had scooped up the three-hundred-dollar tickets for this event alone. I had decided to do The Waverly chicken potpie. I'd made it on *The Martha Stewart Show* and everyone ate it up. It seemed like a safe play for an audience like this. The Best of the Best was slated to take place the next evening at the American Airlines Arena, home to the Miami Heat basketball team. It crossed my mind that since I had the afternoon to spare, maybe I should go check out the venue. On the other hand, I'd only made my potpie about four thousand times. There were plenty more distracting ways to kill an afternoon in South Beach, so I split from the hotel, leaving a Japanese TV crew to ponder whether they should roll tape and give chase to this very famous "personality" from New York, wandering out into the late-day sun in his purple chef badge.

I strolled the footpath along the beach until I ran into a crowd queued up outside an enormous tent on the sand. I had discovered the festival's very own Burger Bash, hosted by the irrepressible Rachael Ray. I approached the heavily fortified entrance where a security guard took one look at my badge and shook his head no. Apparently my badge was the wrong color. Luckily, a friend of mine sauntering in through the VIP entrance saw me, and with a few quick words, I had access.

Inside the oppressively steamy tent, top chefs from around the country were frantically grilling up patties for bragging rights to who has the best burger in the USA. I felt a pang of resentment, since apparently The Waverly's "Best Burger" in *Time Out New York* did not even rate an invitation to compete. On the other hand, I hadn't eaten all day, so I put aside my petty jealousies and scarfed down four extravagantly delicious entries, trying not to think about what bacon a dozen ways and a ton of Gruyère might be doing to my cholesterol count. My protein quota more than met, I decided to head back to my hotel for a refreshing dip. I changed into my swimsuit and hit the pool.

"Jaaahhhn-eeee, whazzup!" I had barely gotten my hair wet when I recognized several fellow "personalities" from the city who had a bottle of Jagermeister going. Spring Break was in full swing. I really should have accepted their generous offer to join in, but green liqueurs do not agree with me, and besides, in truth I was starting to worry a little about my task for tomorrow. I politely declined and a few moments later, slipped back to my room while the sun was still high in the sky.

I slept like shit, tossing and turning all night, and woke up the next morning in full panic mode. I've promised eight hundred perfectly crafted, miniature versions of The Waverly potpie, and it's been three months since I've discussed so much as a single ingredient with the food people from the festival. I fear a disaster in the making, so I grab a chef's coat I had packed to throw over my jeans and T-shirt, and find my way back to the festival hotel, where a complimentary shuttle is waiting to take people to the American Airlines Arena. There are all of about three of us on the bus and it is air-conditioned like a meat locker. I look out of the scratched glass window and recognize Bobby Flay getting into a bright white shiny Lexus. I guess he's not taking the shuttle.

We arrive at the arena and are unceremoniously dumped on a loading dock. A pleasant fellow with a headset radios ahead and a few moments later we are met by someone else in a headset who leads us into the bowels of the arena. After what seems like an interminably long walk, we arrive in the kitchen. It's the size of an airplane hangar. It has enough space to house however many cooks and staff it takes to make hot dogs, pizza, and fries for eighteen thousand fans. The festival staff has cordoned off twenty individual spaces where my fellow chefs and I will have all day to do our thing. Only none of my fellow chefs are anywhere to be seen. I am led to space number fourteen and met by a young woman with a Motorola walkie-talkie and a staff badge. She has three young people with her in chef's coats embroidered with the words "Miami Culinary Institute." I am introduced to Natalie, Brendan, and Georgi from Croatia. They will be my prep team. The staff woman exits stage left.

As my interns look to me for direction, I get this terrible helpless feeling. Eight hundred miniatures potpies from scratch is a tall order. I'm in an unfamiliar kitchen and I don't even know where to start. What's more, where are Bobby and Emeril and Rocco? I'm starting to feel like the kid in third grade who wears his Halloween costume to class only to find out the party's been canceled!

A six-foot-high hotel cart called a Queen Mary appears out of no-where trucking in all the ingredients I had requisitioned, scaled up to eight hundred by a faceless person to whom I'd sent my potpie recipe by e-mail three months ago. I checked the cart. Fifty pounds of chicken; twenty-five pounds of carrots, celery, onions; a fifty-pound bag of flour; twelve gallons of heavy cream, twelve pounds of butter—yep, it's all there. I put Natalie and Brendan to work dicing the carrots, celery, and onions and ordained Georgi from Croatia my butcher assistant. I gave him a quick primer on how to bone and defat a chicken thigh in fifteen seconds or less. The production line began.

After a while I found myself wondering how the other chefs were going to be prepared on time. Then it hit me—they were experienced at these affairs—they must have shipped their food down prepped in advance. And it made perfect sense; they weren't here to cook, they were here to entertain. Only no one bothered to tell me. Could I feel any more foolish? There was no time to think about it, though. I fired up the braiser, which is basically the largest electric frying pan you have ever seen, about as big as a pool table, only it has a basket that tips away from the heat source so you can really load it up. I filled it with water and got it boiling and started throwing chicken parts in to be rapidly poached. "Faster, Georgi," I exhorted him at the cutting board, but his butcher skills were as clumsy as his English because next thing I know the poor bastard has nearly cut his thumb off. Now I feel really rotten because I've got fifty pounds of chicken to poach and this kid, who just wants to help, looks like he might faint from the sight of his own blood. I hustle over to a pile of kitchen towels by one of the stations and start to grab one when I hear a voice call out, "Hey, asshole, where you think you're going with that?" I'm hot and angry and nervous, but when I look up I see that the guy is huge and, from the looks of it, not someone to be reckoned with.

"Just one, OK?" I slip away unscathed.

We get Georgi patched up and back to work. I have Natalie blanch the peas and carrots in a vat of boiling, salted water and then shock them with ice water. Brendan gets going on the pearl onions. Meanwhile, I start punching out eight hundred little rounds of frozen puff pastry for the tops of the pie, while the chicken cooks. My hands are raw and swollen from the steel cookie cutter I'm using on the pastry. We throw several trays into a convection oven preheated to 425 degrees. Puff pastry, with its large quantity of butter, needs to be cooked quickly and at a formidable temperature. I sidetrack to oversee another round of braising chicken and when I return, either someone has messed with the oven (I glare over at towel guy) or its thermostat is way off. My first four trays are a melted, steamy hot, runny mess of emulsified flour and butter. Garbage. We reload and I personally stand guard over the oven and get through a dozen trays. Mercifully, the little buttery rounds come out fine this time, resembling flakey, golden edible coins. Now we're getting somewhere.

The last of the chicken is done and I've got buckets of vegetables sautéing in butter when, out of nowhere, a frantic crowd swirls into the kitchen. There are about a dozen interns in crisp white coats surrounding someone, followed by a camera crew led by a lovely young TV reporter type with a microphone waving in her hand. I recognize David Pasternak, the esteemed chef of Esca in New York, in the center of the ruckus. He marches into his station, which is right next to mine, like he has done this drill a thousand times before. Large ice coolers appear as if by magic and in a flash he is scooping out beautiful whole sea bass, rich and clear-eyed, their scales glistening in the bright lights of the camera. A second A/V crew appears and aims its digital camera over the first crew as David deftly guts and fillets a large bass, all the while speaking into the camera in what appears to be the calmest of tones, just a glint of a smile crossing his face as he wields his razor-sharp knife and eviscerates the fish. Esca is a superior restaurant and even I am taken by David's handiwork. My reverie is broken by a sinewy-looking dude with a headset who steps into my space and asks if I can "keep it down." He wants me to lower the volume on my sizzling braiser full of vegetables. Apparently the molecular chemistry of fat, heat, and carbohydrates is interfering with the sound guy. I shrug. This is supposed to be Food TV. A few realistic sound effects can only enhance the experience.

Three hours later, my three newly minted sous chefs and I are high above the basketball court of the American Airlines Arena in a VIP suite scooping out dollops of steaming, perfectly prepared potpie mix into three-inch tinfoil cups lined with buttery puff pastry. Representatives of two highly regarded wineries from the Napa Valley have joined us and are serving up samples. I've changed into my Indy-esque chef coat and I'm greeting a steady stream of guests who pop in for bites of potpie as they study The Waverly menus I've brought along for the event. Filling the arena where Ewing held off Mourning in one of the great Knicks-Heat games for the ages, hundreds of hungry, food-crazed fans are circulating from one skybox to the next. I'm in the company of Alfred Portale of Gotham Bar & Grill, Dewey LoSasso of North One 10 in Miami, and Karen DeMasco from Craft, in New York. The legendary Masaharu Morimoto is doing his Iron Chef thing in a suite alongside Scott Conant, Michael Lomonaco, and Kerry Simon, all entertaining their own disciples. And then there's me. And for one fleeting moment, as I look out over the arena floor, I think this is pretty fucking cool. All it took was ten hours of backbreaking labor and a simple mix of aromatic vegetables and braised, diced chicken combined with a reduction of vermouth, chicken stock, herbs, and heavy cream with a tiny bit of roux to get me here.

I decided to forgo the complimentary shuttle back to my no-star hotel. Instead, I jumped a cab and headed over to The Raleigh, a place I liked for its soothing, understated charm. A chicken salad sandwich sounded good, and maybe a chilled glass of Prosecco? The taxi glided into the roundabout. I overtipped the cabbie and strolled in. An enormous, remarkably fashionable crowd milled about the lobby with fruity, martini-like drinks. A velvet rope blocked off the entire bar area. Then I remembered my badge. I walked up to the bronzed bouncer on the velvet rope. "Sorry pal," he said, shooing me away.

I flashed my purple festival ID tag in his face like a crisp C-note. "That's no good here," he said. "Private dinner for Jean-Georges. Gonna have to ask you to leave." I stared helplessly. Wrong-colored badge again. Access denied.

I walked back to my hotel and dragged myself upstairs. I settled into the Naugahyde easy chair and called down to room service, enjoying my view of the industrial-size air-conditioning generator on the roof next door. It took an hour and a half to get my sandwich delivered. I was on the 6:15 a.m. back to New York the next morning.

Twelve hours later I'm sitting on the steps of The Waverly enjoying my usual espresso. Bank Street is especially quiet and the air mild for late February in the city. I linger just a bit longer than normal before strolling in. It can't be seven p.m. and already we are hopping. I pass the bar where Doug is uncorking a nice little 2003 Pauillac for a customer to wash down his $55 mac and cheese with. "Evening, Chef," our waiter Andre greets me, as he shaves some truffle over the customer's steaming plate of noodles. "How was Miami?"

"Perfect." I nod cordially, walking through the dining room. It's good to be back. Everything seems to be in order. Tables are full. The waitstaff is reciting the specials. Salman Rushdie is enjoying an early supper with a spectacular young woman. As I walk toward the kitchen I feel someone grab the sleeve of my white coat.

"Son, do you work here"? A very old lady dressed in a vintage dress, only on her it was original, not vintage, tugs again at me. "Yes," I say. "I do work here."

"Well," she announces regally, "I first had this chicken potpie in 1961 on a date, and it tastes even better tonight. Will you please send my compliments to the chef."

I lean over and whisper to her conspiratorially. "Ma'am, I'll do just that."

She squeezes my hand with gratitude, and the two old biddies resume their conversation. I detour back to the bar. "Doug," I call out over the crowd that had grown to two deep. "The ladies at 314? What are they drinking?

"Chablis," he says with a smile.

"Hunhh?" I reply. "Do we serve Chablis?"

"I substituted. Château Lamothe 2004."

"Mmmm, nice." I nod. If all it took was a potpie and a very elegant faux Chablis to make these two neighborhood customers happy, then I can rest easy, knowing we are doing something right. I sneak back through the dining room, unnoticed, and return to the kitchen. The heat hits me like a sauna. I grab three dupes as they clatter out of the printer. "Two chickens, two steaks, whole fish, c'mon!" Plates are backing up on the pass. Angel has all twelve burners flaming. Emil pokes his head in disapprovingly. I recognize that look. No falling behind. "Let's go, Papi," I call out, wiping my head with a hand towel. It is time to get busy.